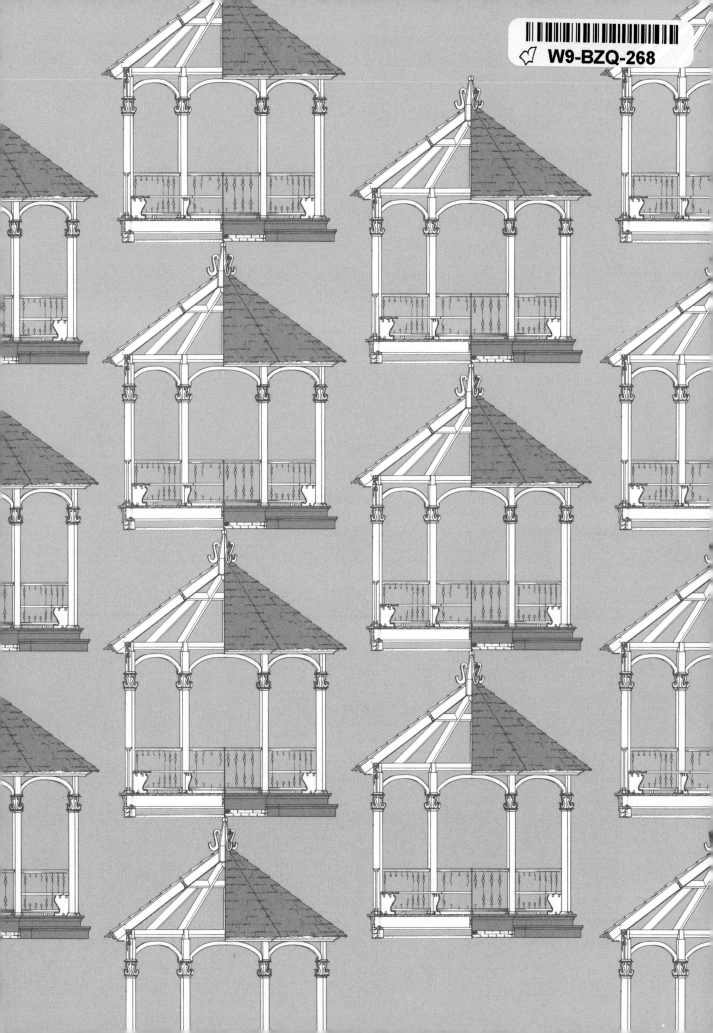

Popular Mechanics

do-it-yourself encyclopedia

GUIDE TO OUTDOOR STRUCTURES

HEARST DIRECT BOOKS

NEW YORK

This book is published with the consent and cooperation of POPULAR MECHANICS Magazine.

POPULAR MECHANICS Staff:
Editor-in-Chief: Joe Oldham
Managing Editor: Bill Hartford
Graphics Director: Bryan Canniff
Automotive Editor: Tony Swan
Home and Shop Editor: Steven Willson
Electronics/Photography Editor: Stephen A. Booth
Boating/Outdoors Editor: Joe Skorupa
Science Editor: Timothy H. Cole
Editorial Production: John Bostonian Jr.

**POPULAR MECHANICS ENCYCLOPEDIA
GUIDE TO OUTDOOR STRUCTURES**

Written by:
    Dan Ramsey
Additional Material by:
    David A. Warren
    Al Gutierrez
Editor:
    C. Edward Cavert
Manufacturing:
    Ron Schoenfeld
Book Design and Production:
    The Bookmaker
    Fairfax, Virginia
Editorial Assistance:
    Wilma Cavert
    Barbara S. Hatheway
Illustrations and Graphic Enhancement:
    Thomas Dahlen
    Guilio Porta

Credits and Acknowledgments

The following individuals and organizations have provided material that has contributed to *Popular Mechanics Guide to Outdoor Structures*:

Illustration of metal fasteners in Chapter 1, *Building Outdoor Projects*, (page 21) courtesy of Wolman Division, Koppers Co., Inc.

Chaise lounge project in Chapter 2, *Outdoor Furniture*, by David A. Warren, design and construction by Steve Presenza, photographs by Mike Rosamond with graphic enhancement by Thom Dahlen. Settee and picnic table projects by Al Gutierrez, photos and plan drawings by Media Management Group.

Photographs of the backyard play center in Chapter 3, *Outdoor Play Equipment*, by Mike Rosamond. Design and construction of the project by Steve Presenza. Plan drawings by Gerard Latada. Material written by David A. Warren.

Plans for slat fence and wooden gate projects in Chapter 4, *Fence and Gate Designs*, provided by Southern Forest Products Association. Other drawings courtesy Sears Roebuck & Co. (page 54), Western Wood Products Association (page 55) and California Redwood Association (page 55).

Plans for the ground-level and raised deck projects in Chapter 5, *Deck Design and Construction*, provided by Southern Forest Products Association. Hot-tub deck plans and deck construction details (page 57) from California Redwood Association.

Metal shed drawings in Chapter 6, *Sheds and Storage Buildings*, courtesy of Sears Roebuck & Co. Plans for the wooden shed, trash can storage and potting shed from Southern Forest Products Association. Garden storage shed and small storage barn plans from American Plywood Association.

Plans for the square gazebo in Chapter 7, *Gazebos and Decorative Structures*, from Southern Forest Products Association. The hexagon gazebo plans were provided by Western Wood Products Association. The ornate Tiffany Gazebo is from Sun Designs, Delafield, Wisconsin.

Material and drawings in Chapter 8, *Brick and Masonry Projects*, provided by the Brick Institute of America, Reston, Virginia.

Material and photographs in Chapter 9, *Swimming Pools and Spas*, provided by National Spa and Pool Institute, Alexandria, Virginia. Drawings in Chapter 9 are from Swimming Pools, by Bill Tanler, copyright 1984. Used by permission of the publisher, HPBooks, Inc.

Plans in Chapter 10, *Garage Design and Construction*, and plans for *Barns and Pole Buildings* in Chapter 11 obtained from National Plan Service, Inc. More detailed plans of these projects can be obtained by writing National Plan Service at 435 W. Fullerton Ave., Elmhurst, Illinois 60126.

Contents

Introduction

No matter how much space you have in your house, it always seems that it is never quite enough to store your tools, toys and other possessions. As your leisure time increases, you'll want to have special places for recreational activities. The purpose of this book is to show you how to expand your living and storage space with outdoor structures you can build.

An outdoor structure is any project that expands the living space outside the walls of your home. For example, a lounge offers a resting spot in the shade, a fence gives added privacy, and a storage shed offers a convenient place for your tools and toys. Play equipment provides an outdoor outlet for the natural energy level of young children.

Outdoor structures are also fun to build. With simple tools and clear instructions, you can easily construct most of the projects shown here in an afternoon or a weekend. Most outdoor structures require only rough carpentry where 1/8 inch isn't as critical as in cabinetmaking and interior furniture projects. In fact, many outdoor projects can be built by the whole family with children learning along with parents.

Additional Help

The material in this book expands on the specific instructions and projects you'll find throughout the 27 volumes of your *Popular Mechanics Do-it-Yourself Encyclopedia*. There's a detailed guide at the end of this book that will help you locate other projects and information in your *Encyclopedia*.

In Chapter 1 there is a review of basic outdoor construction methods from laying out the foundation, through concrete and masonry work to rough and finish carpentry. You'll learn the best way to dig a post hole or to put in a storage shed foundation. There are also helpful tips on laying brick and a review of other masonry skills. You'll review the basics of horizontal and vertical framing in working with wood.

There is ample material throughout the 27 volumes of your *Popular Mechanics Do-it-Yourself Encyclopedia* that you can review to brush up on your basic building skills or to review your knowledge of tools and construction techniques. You will want to review the basics of hand tools in Volume 12 and power tools in Volume 19. The material in Volume 6 about working with concrete and concrete blocks will give you additional help as you read the material in this book. Finally, you'll want to look again at the introduction to carpentry in Volume 5 and the short course in joinery in Volume 14 to review these essential skills.

Chapter 2 begins the specific outdoor structure projects offering step-by-step instructions and illustrations for building practical and easy outdoor furniture. This chapter will show you how to build projects such as a chaise lounge, outdoor settee and a picnic table.

Additional outdoor furniture projects are explained in Volume 16 of your *Encyclopedia*, and you'll find more picnic table plans in Volume 18. You may also want to look at the planter projects in Volume 18.

Chapter 3 includes projects for building outdoor play equipment. It gives plans and material lists for constructing a backyard play center with a sandbox, monkey bars, balance beam, seesaw and climbing platform. There are also plans for a playhouse you can reclaim in future years as a storage shed.

Other projects for children's outdoor playground equipment are in Volume 18 of the *Encyclopedia*.

Chapter 4 gives a variety of fence materials and designs. Step-by-step instructions guide you through the process from digging post holes through adding a decorative gate.

This material adds important information and projects to the material about fences in Volume 9 of your *Encyclopedia*.

Chapter 5 shows you how to build a deck in your own yard. It includes plans and materials for a ground-level deck, raised deck and hot tub deck.

You'll find this material a valuable addition to the basic deck construction tips and projects in Volume 7 of the *Encyclopedia*.

Chapter 6 illustrates how to install metal storage sheds as well as how to construct a wooden storage shed, garden storage shed, small storage barn, trash can storage, and a potting shed. It includes complete materials lists and ideas for customizing plans.

Other projects for building yard structures like these are explained in Volume 27 of your *Encyclopedia*.

Chapter 7 features gazebos and other decorative structures. You'll learn how to locate and plan your own gazebo as well as how to construct a square gazebo, attached gazebo, popular hexagon gazebo and a decorative Tiffany gazebo. Clear illustrations make the job easier.

Chapter 8 shows you how to add a decorative flair to an outdoor project with mortarless brick work and other masonry projects.

In Chapter 9 you will be told how to plan for and design a family swimming pool or other decorative yard pool. If a pool is too ambitious a project, the ideas for back-yard spas may be more in keeping with your needs. You'll also find out about some of the precautions you must take when planning and building a spa or pool on your property.

To supplement this material, you'll find information on swimming pool maintenance and swimming pool improvements in Volume 23 of the *Encyclopedia*.

Chapter 10 will guide you through the planning and construction of a garage. It can help you even if your just planning to add on to your present garage for more space. Specifically, this chapter includes plans, materials and instructions for building a single car garage, double car garage, and triple car garage. You'll also learn how to install and repair overhead garage doors.

You'll find these projects a useful addition to the garage projects explained in Volume 11 of your *Encyclopedia*.

Chapter 11 covers barns of all sizes and features tips and instructions from foundation to wall to roof construction. Most important, it gives you the plans and materials lists for a 12×12 ft., 12×16 ft., and 12×20 ft. gambrel barns and a 28×40 ft. pole building.

Tools and Materials

Outdoor structures can be built with nothing more than a hammer and a handsaw. The do-it-yourselfer, however, has a variety of labor-saving tools to select from to make the task easier and the construction more structurally sound. You don't need a complete workshop to build outdoor structures, but the basic hand tools such as a hammer, saw, drill, wrench, chisel and plane are almost essential. Power circular saws and power bench tools will most certainly speed up the project. The correct tool, well maintained, can make the job of building outdoor structures easier.

Just as it is important to select the right tool for the job, it is equally important to use the right kind of materials. For good materials, choose a trusted retailer. You probably already have experience with many building material stores, lumber yards and hardware stores in your area.

Shop around for the best price. Some dealers may offer a discount for cash while others may offer free delivery of the material to your site. Paying a little more for a load of brick that is delivered to your yard may well be worth the extra cost when you compare it to the cost of repairs to your car—or to your back!

Review the materials you'll need for your project. Is it primarily a wood, concrete or a hardware project? If it's wood, do you plan to use naturally decay-resistant wood such as cedar or redwood or are you going to use self-treated or pressure-treated lumber? For concrete projects, can you use ready-to-mix concrete or do you need a truck to deliver it?

You will find specific help on selection and using hand tools and power tools in your *Popular Mechanics Do-it-Yourself Encyclopedia*. Most of the hand tools you'll use are covered in Volume 12. The most common power tools you'll use are the circular saw (with tips in Volume 6) and the portable electric drill (Volume 8). You'll also want to read the material about keeping your power tools in shape in Volume 19.

The sections about wood and woodworking in Volume 26 of the *Encyclopedia* are a good review of the characteristics of different types of wood and wood products. There's also material in Volume 26 about the techniques for using materials lists to estimate the amount of wood to buy for your project that you'll want to refer to often as you plan the next outdoor structure you'll build.

Building Outdoor Projects

In this chapter you'll find a basic course in planning, carpentry, masonry and tool safety for building outdoor structures. Before you begin any of the projects shown later in this book, you'll want to sharpen your skills and basic knowledge in these areas. You'll find additional information and helpful hints throughout the 27 volumes of your *Popular Mechanics Do-it-Yourself Encyclopedia*, starting with a review of **Hand Tools** in Volume 12 and **Power Tools** in Volume 19. Follow up your review of basic **Carpentry** in Volume 5 by reading again the short course in **Joinery** that you'll find in Volume 14. Finally, you can supplement the material about basic masonry construction given here with the material about **Concrete** and **Concrete Block** work that you'll find in Volume 5.

PLANNING OUTDOOR STRUCTURES

There are many important considerations when planning and building an outdoor structure, whether it be a barn or a bird house. Knowing and following them can help ensure the success of your project.

The first consideration, of course, is to check your local building codes. This will tell you, for example, how deep the concrete footing for your project must be. Don't rely on second-hand information about building code requirements; it's no fun to find out that the concrete base for your wall should have been deeper—*after* you've already finished it.

Discuss the location of your outdoor project with the family. You might want the outdoor play equipment for your children in line of sight of a kitchen window, while your family may prefer to have your garden shed tucked out of sight around a corner of the house or behind some shrubbery.

The next consideration is weather. While you're snug and warm inside throughout the year, your outdoor structure may be exposed to below-zero cold, intense heat, high humidity and

strong winds. These weather changes can dramatically shorten the life of your structure.

Weather is a special consideration when selecting materials and finishes. Decking that will have a three-month snow covering will need extra waterproofing treatment. A tool storage building in an area of heavy rains may require a gutter system with splash blocks to keep water runoff from seeping around doors and foundation. Wood furniture that is exposed to hot and humid weather should be treated with an anti-blistering finish.

Another consideration is permanency. Is it important that you are able to relocate your outdoor structure? Do you move frequently? Can you easily store your outdoor furniture during the off season? Should you be able to move your lawn furniture conveniently to capture the sun or the shade? Do you want to be able to dismantle your outdoor structure?

You can design portability into your outdoor project. Consider adding an axle and wheels to outdoor furniture and cooking units. By installing hinge fasteners at the corners of a small outdoor storage building, you can fold it flat. You can also construct a sturdy four-wheel cart to put under a picnic table, large bench, planter or other structure for moving.

The design drawing helps you visualize the finished project.

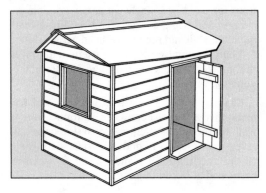

Making Plans

Plans are available for every type of outdoor structure project. Most do-it-yourselfers, however, have some modification they want to make: move a gate, add an extra stairway, build a heavier bench, widen the garage for additional storage. That's why it is useful for you to draw your own plans. You can construct a project from any of the plans in this book just as they are or you can make modifications according to your own specific tastes.

Another good reason for designing your own plans is that you'll reduce the amount of waste and the cost of your project. Whether you are studying stock plans or drawing your own, knowing how to read plans will save you time, money and frustration.

There are three kinds of plans for a project. They are the design drawing, the dimension plan and the three-view plan. The *design drawing* is a rough diagram of what the project will look like when completed. You can sketch it freehand on a sheet of scrap paper to help visualize the project. The *dimension plan* takes the design drawing one step further. Draw these plans with a ruler, a T-square and a draftsman's triangle for both perspective and accuracy. You can draw it on drafting paper or blank typing paper. The plan should include specific dimensions of the project as a unit, but remember that most projects cannot be built from just a dimension plan.

The three-view or *elevation plan* carries the dimension plan one step further, sketching and giving dimensions for three sides of the project: front, top and end. The elevation plan is not necessary for constructing a fence, but it is vital to building a lawn chair, storage shed or garage. It offers specific dimensions for selecting and cutting materials.

Some projects can benefit from even more planning. If you are designing a project made from expensive materials, use thick paper cutouts to make sure the components will match. This works especially well for small projects such as a decorative planter or bird house. You can lay out the cutouts to determine how to place the parts on the material with the least amount of waste.

Most projects will benefit from some type of layout before construction. You can even build decks and larger structures around a board and batten layout. To do this, lay strings between corner posts to ensure accurate dimensions and be sure it's square before building. For larger projects, such as a shed or greenhouse attached to the side of a house, you can outline it using 1×2s to make sure that it aesthetically matches the lines of the house.

FOUNDATIONS

There are three basic types of foundations you'll need to know about for your outdoor structures: post foundations, pier foundations and continuous foundations. Each of these requires careful planning and layout to ensure that your structure will not only have a solid base of support, but that it will be built on a level and square base.

Post Foundations

The foundation for a post is simple. It requires surrounding the post with materials to both brace and protect. Usually, this means installing a gravel base in the hole for drainage, bracing the post with wood cross members in weak soils and filling the hole around the post with packing. Packing can be concrete, rock or gravel, depending on the soil and elements. Concrete is more stable but it can heave and damage the structure if not extended below the frost line.

The dimension plan offers specific dimensions and sizes on a floor-plan layout of the project.

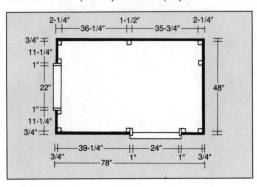

Elevation plan combines the design and dimension plan, giving horizontal and vertical measurements.

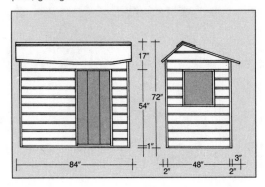

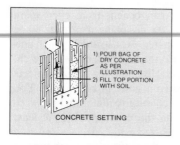

Typical fence post hole will have gravel in the bottom for drainage with the post held in concrete.

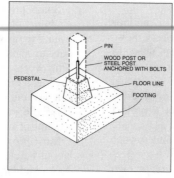

Pier foundation and post footing.

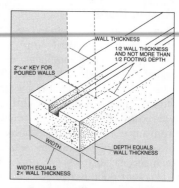

Footing for continuous foundation.

Pier Foundations

Pier foundations are easy to install because you can purchase them as pier blocks. Install piers or large reinforced concrete blocks above ground by pouring a concrete footing in a hole and installing the pier above it. The post then sits on top of the pier. Place bolts and brackets between the footing, pier and post to reinforce and stabilize.

You can also build piers by combining the footing, pier and post in one unit. Set a hollow cardboard cylinder into the ground, install appropriate reinforcement bars and pour concrete to the correct height. Once the concrete has cured, peel the cardboard away.

Continuous Foundations

More complex, yet more sturdy, is the continuous foundation. Continuous foundations, in most cases, are made with concrete blocks.

If you are using concrete block for your foundation, find the outside wall corners and then pour the footing and lay the concrete blocks. Run a cord tightly between corners to outline the outside of the block wall and mark with a chalk stick or chalkline. Lay the first course of blocks without mortar around the perimeter to determine joint spacing. You'll also find out now if you'll have to cut any blocks. Use a small scrap piece of ⅜-in. plywood as a spacer to allow for mortar, make necessary spacing adjustments, then mark each joint on the footing. Check the outdoor structure plan for any openings you'll need for such things as crawl space entrances, vents, drains or utilities before you start laying the blocks.

Poured concrete foundations are more complex. They require forms to hold the wet concrete until it hardens or cures.

Continuous foundation constructed of concrete blocks. Anchor bolts are used to attach sill plate to the foundation.

Poured concrete continuous foundation requires forms. Bracing keeps forms in place until concrete cures.

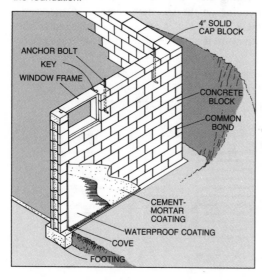

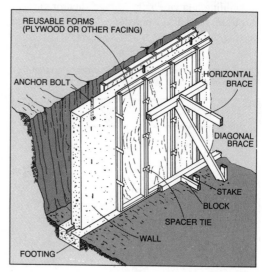

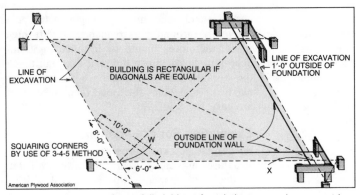

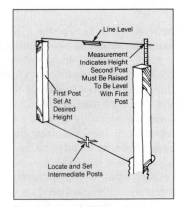

A carefully laid out foundation can make any outdoor project easier.

Fence posts of different heights are installed with a line level.

After you have poured the concrete, leave the forms in place until you are certain that the concrete is hard. Concrete doesn't dry by the evaporation of water but by a chemical change. It takes about ten days for concrete to dry enough to remove the forms. During this period of curing, keep the concrete moist and out of the sun. Place cloth, paper or straw over the concrete. Sprinkle this cover with water every day; more frequently on hot, dry days. Let the concrete "season" this way for at least a week; two weeks or more of seasoning are needed for slabs poured for garages or shed floors.

Foundation Layout

Laying out a foundation is the critical beginning in constructing outdoor structures. By making sure that the foundation is square and level, you'll ensure that later construction is both more accurate and easier.

First, make sure your structure complies with local building regulations and is sufficiently within your lot lines. If property lines are in question, have a city, county, or private surveyor come to mark your boundaries. Your tax assessor or mortgage banker can recommend a surveyor. Regulations may require that your structure be 5, 10, 20 or more feet from a lot line (this is called setback). It's better to check this now rather than find out later that the county building inspector requires you to move your new structure.

Also consider natural drainage. This is especially important for structures such as a barn, fence or greenhouse. If drainage is poor you can move the structure or improve drainage at the site you selected by sloping or by adding collection and distribution systems.

Once you've decided on proper placement and adequate drainage, you can begin the physical layout. Locate each outside corner and drive small stakes into the ground. Drive a nail in the top of each of these stakes and attach a string between them. Check to see if the corners are square by measuring 6 ft. along one side and 8 ft. along the other, then measure diagonally

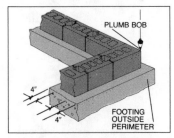

Laying building block on cement footing.

Sill plate is installed on top of the foundation. Vents or screens are used in place of some blocks in the foundation wall.

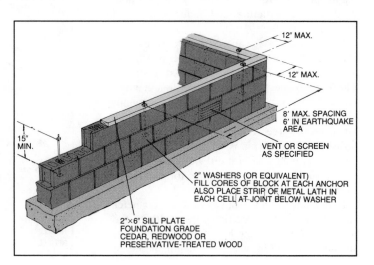

between these two points. The diagonal measurement should be 10 ft. if the corner is square.

Next, drive 2×2-in. or larger stakes at each corner. If you are laying out a foundation, locate these stakes 3 to 4 ft. outside the actual foundation line and attach 1×6-in. batter boards so their top edges are all at the same height and level. Then stretch a string line across tops of opposite batter boards and, using a plumb bob, adjust so that it is exactly over the center of the corner stakes. If you are laying out a line for a structure that doesn't need a foundation, such as a fence, simply string a line between the corner stakes or from batter boards a few feet beyond the stakes.

Next, check for level. Remember that the top of a foundation must be level around the entire perimeter of the structure. The best way to verify level is with a surveyor's level if you have access to and knowledge of using one. Otherwise, lay a long piece of lumber between the corner posts or batter boards and place a carpenter or masonry level on top of it. If your foundation line is long, you may have to do this leveling procedure in sections.

PREPARING THE SITE

An essential step in any outdoor construction is to prepare the site. This can be as simple as using a post-hole digger to excavate for your fence posts to having someone with a backhoe dig a deep trench for a continuous poured-concrete footing and foundation.

Excavating for Posts

Posts are the foundations for fences, decks, gazebos and other outdoor structures. Excavating for posts is critical because a poor post hole weakens the structure and reduces both its safety and its life.

Install posts 4 ft. apart for structures that carry weight, such as decks and other platforms, and 6 to 8 ft. apart for non-load-bearing fences. The heavier the fence, the closer together the posts should be. You can dig post holes manually with a post-hole digger that cuts and lifts the dirt from the hole. You can also use a powered post-hole digger. This is an auger that screws into the ground and lifts dirt out. Augers normally require two operators, one for each side, to maintain stability.

Depending on the soil, post hole diameter should be two to three times the width of the post. For example, the hole for a 4×4-in. post should be 8 to 12 in. wide. The depth should be

approximately one-third the height of the post above the ground plus 6 inches. A 6-ft.-high fence, therefore, should be installed in 30-in.-deep post holes. Since the post does not touch the bottom, the post can be 8 ft. long. Dig narrower post holes for metal fence posts that are only 2 to 3 in. wide.

Excavating For Foundations

Sheds, garages and barns are heavier outdoor structures and carry greater loads than a fence or deck. To dispense this additional weight, install continuous foundations along the perimeter of the structure.

Poured-concrete footings are popular and practical. Excavating for a poured-concrete footing requires that you remove the soil the width of the footing *and* the work area. The footing should be at least twice as wide as the foundation. The working area beyond this depends upon the structure and the soil. If you use concrete blocks for the foundation above the footing, you need a wide work area. Harder soils can serve as the outside perimeter of the footing and, in many cases, eliminate both the form board and the work area.

You can cast the footing and foundation in concrete as one unit. This requires installing reinforcement bar or rebar to hold the added concrete together under stress. When excavating for a concrete foundation, the work area can be narrower. Install forms in this work area and brace them to the outside of the excavation.

Excavating for a foundation. Note working space necessary on both sides of the footing trench.

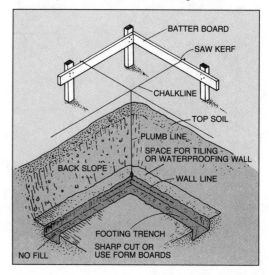

Digging the excavation with a shovel for even a small foundation can be a long and tedious, back-tiring job—especially if you're digging in hard clay soil. If you have a large outdoor structure you need a foundation or footing trench for, or if you have to go fairly deep to get below the frost line in your area, you may want to have this part of the job done for you by a professional with a backhoe.

BUILDING WITH CONCRETE

Concrete is a mixture of cement and aggregate (gravel and sand) mixed with water. You'll need concrete for most of your outdoor building projects: fence post foundations, outdoor fireplaces, garage floors, walks and garden pools.

The information here is just a review of the more detailed instructions for various outdoor projects that you'll find in your volumes of the *Popular Mechanics Do-it-Yourself Encyclopedia*. Different kinds of post foundations for fences are in Volume 9; You'll find more information about footings for decks in Volume 6. The section about concrete, also in Volume 6, gives detailed instructions for a poured concrete slab that you would use for a garage floor or shed in your outdoor structure building projects.

Planning Concrete Construction

Any concrete construction is done in steps. These include preparing the grade or base for the material, building the forms, placing the concrete in the forms, finishing the concrete, and

Mason's tools are specifically designed to make bricklaying easier.

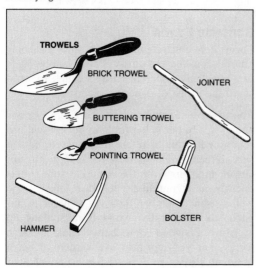

curing the concrete. Materials used include crushed stone for the base; dimension lumber, plywood or hardboard for the forms; 2×4s for form stakes; the concrete itself; material such as plastic sheeting, burlap and straw to cover the concrete during curing.

For small jobs such as fence post foundations, you can buy ready-to-mix concrete in bags or you can buy the cement and aggregate and mix the concrete yourself. Be prepared for lots of hard, dirty work. Concrete has a short work time—usually an hour—so mix only enough to work in that period of time.

For large jobs, it's easier to order already-mixed concrete you can have delivered to your job. Most home centers and hardware stores do not sell already-mixed concrete, but some rent concrete mixers if you want to tackle the mixing job yourself. For small jobs, such as post holes you can mix the concrete is a plastic tub, wheelbarrow or simply on a sheet of plywood.

Poured concrete work—such as a foundation, driveway, walk or patio—usually is governed by local building codes. You may also need a building permit to pour concrete.

Estimating Concrete Needs.

Quantities of concrete are measured in cubic yards or simply *yards*. For foundations, slabs or footings multiply the length by the width then by the depth or thickness. Divide this volume by 27 to get the number of cubic yards you'll need.

Ready-mixed concrete is sold by the yard. Premixed formulas you buy by the bag in a store—concrete, mortar, and sand—contain about ⅓ yard in each 80 lb. bag.

Concrete Selection

Portland cement is the basic ingredient for all concrete and mortar. Cement binds the other materials together into a strong, watertight composition. "Portland" is not a trade name. It refers to the type of cement in general use.

The next ingredient in making concrete is sand or *fine aggregate*. The sand must be free of dirt, clay or vegetable matter (such as leaves). Sand from ocean beaches is not satisfactory because it contains salt. Test the sand for purity by placing a small amount of it in a glass of water and stir. Let the sand settle to the bottom of the glass. If the water is only slightly discolored, the sand is clean enough. Dirty sand will give you poor concrete.

The third ingredient for concrete is crushed stone or pebbles. This material is called *coarse aggregate* and ranges in size from ½ in. to 2 in. depending on the job you're using it for. When working on a thin wall, the size of the coarse aggregate should not be more than one-third the thickness of the thinnest section of the wall. This coarse aggregate should also be clean and free of imperfections.

Pure water completes the list of materials needed for making concrete. A good rule to follow is to use only water fit for drinking to mix with cement. Dirt or other matter in the water will produce inferior concrete. Never use salt water.

Mixing Concrete

The proportion of cement, sand, gravel and water used for mixing concrete depends on the kind of work you're doing and the condition of the sand and gravel. These two materials are seldom completely free of moisture, so take this into account when adding water.

The strength of concrete depends on the union of the water and cement to form a paste which, when hard, will bind the particles of sand and gravel together. It's important that the proper portions of water and cement be maintained. The best all-around formula for concrete you mix yourself is 3 parts gravel mix, 2 parts sand and 1 part cement.

After you mix these ingredients thoroughly, run a trowel across the mound of the mixture. The trowel should leave a smooth and solid track indicating that everything has been evenly mixed. You have to guess at the amount of water, but you will know when the mix is right

Brick and stone walkways are best installed over a concrete base.

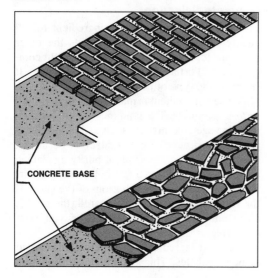

CONCRETE BASE

by its consistency: like cake batter or fairly stiff whipped cream. Too much water will make the mixture weak; too little water will make the mixture difficult to float and trowel to a smooth finish. Adding water to the mixture after it has been placed in the forms will weaken the cement. Complete all mixing before the concrete is poured and finished.

Concrete that has been properly mixed can be poured into a form or post hole with ease and packed down until it forms a dense mass.

Premixed Concrete

Although more costly than mixing concrete, sand and gravel yourself, the bagged premixes are convenient, easy to handle and ideal for small jobs where only a yard or two of concrete is needed. There are three types of premixes found in almost all home centers and hardware stores and even some drug stores.

Concrete mix has coarse aggregate (gravel or crushed stone ranging in size from ¼ to 1½ in.) and is used for projects where strength is needed. Since the mixture's strength exceeds 4000 lb. per square inch, it is the best mix to use for walks, patios, fence post foundations and light-support foundations.

Mortar mix has a sand aggregate that will sift through ¼-in. screen mesh. Its strength is 1250 lb. per square inch. Use it for building brick or concrete walls and for tuckpointing damaged mortar joints.

Sand mix has a strength of more than 5000 lb. per square inch. The aggregate is fine—similar to mortar mix—and the material may be used for grouting, patching cracks, tuckpointing, or setting stone goods such as walks or walls.

Concrete Forms

Forms hold concrete in position while it is being poured, finished and cured. Forms can be made of almost any material sturdy enough to withstand the thrust of concrete against it.

Foundation Forms. Wet concrete weighs about 125 lb. per cubic foot, so you should use reinforced forms to retain the concrete until it sets. Green lumber is best because it will not absorb moisture from the concrete and, consequently, it is not likely to warp. If you use well-seasoned lumber, coat it with oil or tar paper to prevent the wood from soaking up moisture. Plywood is excellent for making large forms, but you can also use hardboard when irregular shapes and curves are a part of your design. For larger jobs, such as foundations and retaining walls, you can rent concrete forms.

Plan the size of your forms so you don't have to cut the wood much and you can use the same wood later for other jobs. Build the forms so they can be taken apart easily and without damage to the wood or concrete. Wherever possible, use bolts, screws and clamps rather than nails. If you use nails, use duplex nails so they can be pulled out easily and quickly.

Slab Forms. Dimension lumber (2×4s, 2×6s, 2×8s) generally is used to make forms for driveways, walks, patios and slabs. Boards (1×4s, 1×6s, 1×8s) can also be used for forms for small jobs such as a garden pathway or individual forms for stepping stones. Stake the boards with short lengths of 2×3s or 2×4s.

Control Joints. Slabs of concrete expand and contract as weather changes. This movement, if not controlled, can crack and break the concrete.

Three methods are used to prevent cracking. The simplest: a tool called a *divider* is drawn across the finished concrete, making an indentation about an inch deep. On a sidewalk, for example, you draw the divider across the slab every four feet or so.

A better method uses expansion joints—strips of asphalt material ½ in. thick and 4 in. wide—that you insert into the finished concrete every three or four feet. After it has been poured, slice down into the concrete with a trowel and force a piece of expansion-joint material into the crack; then finish the concrete. You should place an expansion joint against an existing structure, such as a stair step or foundation wall, before placing new concrete against it.

Permanent Forms. Wooden strips or forms sometimes are left in place after the concrete hardens and cures. These forms serve as expansion joints to help prevent concrete from cracking and breaking. Standard expansion-joint material is not necessary against the sides of the forms, although expansion joints may be used at foundation walls, steps or other house parts against which the new concrete butts.

The permanent forms should be made with wood that doesn't rot—redwood, cedar or cypress. Pressure-treated lumber offers some rot resistance, but should be considered a second choice to these natural rot-resistant woods. Never use untreated wood.

BRICK AND MASONRY WORK

Concrete blocks, bricks and building stones are called *masonry*. You can use masonry in many ways in outdoor structures. Garage and storage building foundations can use concrete blocks, brick is good for outdoor fireplaces, and stone makes attractive walkways.

Building With Concrete Blocks

Cinder and concrete blocks are popular outdoor building materials because they are structurally strong, symmetrically pleasing and inexpensive. A comprehensive course on laying concrete blocks is in Volume 6 of the *Popular Mechanics Do-it-Yourself Encyclopedia*.

Standard-weight concrete blocks are made from a mixture of cement, sand and coarse aggregate such as gravel. The mixture is placed in block molds. Lighter-weight blocks use other aggregates such as pumice, shale or cinders. Since these aggregates are of lighter weight, the units are easier to handle. You must, however, comply with local codes if these lighter-weight blocks are used.

The most common hollow-core construction block is labeled 8×8×16 but these dimensions are nominal. The actual size of the block is 7⅝×7⅝×15⅝ in. The ⅜-in. difference is for the mortar that holds the units together. Other block dimensions (nominal size) include blocks that are 4 or 8 inches wide, 4, 8, or 12 inches high and 8 or 16 inches long. For foundations walls, blocks 12 inches high are often used.

Concrete sidewalks need forms, level bed and expansion joints. Strike board smoothes out concrete.

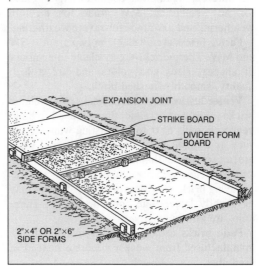

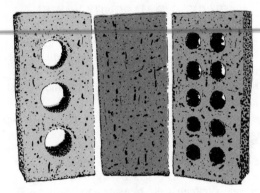

Brick types include solid bricks, which are recommended for general work, and cored bricks which give mortar better holding power.

Building with Brick

Whether your outdoor project is a sweeping walkway, a barbecue or just a small planter, brick can provide an accent to give it a look of permanence and distinction.

Brick construction—with the exception of maintenance and repair—is subject to local codes similar to those governing any outdoor construction. Be sure you check with local authorities before building with brick.

Types of Bricks

Bricks come in a wide variety of sizes, colors and textures. They are also made for interior or exterior use, so you should buy the type that best fits your project.

Common bricks are available in only a few shapes, sizes and colors and are roughly finished. There are three grades of common brick for different weathering conditions. NW grade for no weathering, MW grade for medium weathering and SW grade for severe weathering.

Facing bricks are available in two grades: SW and MW. These bricks are available in a variety of shapes, sizes and colors and are a high quality, smoothly finished brick.

Veneer bricks may be real bricks or simulated bricks (plastic or ceramic) that are used to build veneered walls next to an existing wall surface such as framing and sheathing. Veneered walls are not structural; that is, they aren't designed to support heavy weight such as a roof.

Paving bricks for driveways or walkways may be slightly larger than common bricks. These units are known as *pavers*.

Patio bricks usually are not pavers, but are manufactured from weaker concrete instead of fired clay.

Firebricks are quite different from building bricks. They are manufactured from a clay mixture that will withstand extreme heat. They appear quite dense and heavy compared with building bricks. You'll use firebrick in outdoor fireplaces and barbecues.

Brick Mortar

Patios, walkways and edgings need not be mortared for permanence. If you've leveled the ground and put down two inches of sand, you'll be able to lay brick neatly and quickly. If heaving occurs during the winter, you can repair it by just lifting out a few bricks, leveling the sand and replacing the bricks. You will, however, need to mortar the brick for a wall or fireplace, and you may *want* to mortar a driveway or patio.

There are two ways to get mortar. The simplest is to buy a sack of dry-mix mortar, add water, stir and you're ready for the trowel. One sack of dry-mix is enough for about 50 bricks.

While dry-mix isn't expensive, it does cost more than mortar you can make on your own from its raw materials—Portland cement, sand and hydrated lime.

Mortar should be mixed in small quantities so it doesn't dry out. Enough mortar for 40 bricks can be made from one shovel of Portland cement, 3 shovels of sand and ¼ shovel of hydrated lime.

For 500 bricks, you'll need 1⅓ sacks of Portland cement, 4 sacks of sand and ⅓ sack of hydrated lime. The extra lime can be used on your lawn.

Artificial brick is a brick veneer that is fastened to a horizontal or vertical surface with adhesive. To break brick veneer, score it with a hacksaw and snap it over a straightedge such as a pencil.

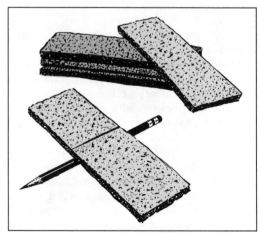

Estimating Brick Needs

Common or standard bricks have a nominal size of $2\frac{3}{4} \times 4\frac{1}{2} \times 8\frac{1}{2}$ inches. Their actual size is $2\frac{1}{4} \times 3\frac{1}{4} \times 8$ inches. The smaller measurement allows for mortar joints. Standard mortar joints are $\frac{3}{8}$ of an inch thick. Larger joint spacing will increase the amount of mortar needed.

A good rule of thumb when estimating brick needs is: You need about 8 bricks per square foot of area. First calculate the area to be bricked—length × width in feet—then multiply by eight.

Bricks arrive at your dealer's yard on pallets of 500, and this is the most economical and efficient way to buy them. For an additional charge, your dealer can deliver the bricks to your site strapped, ready to use when you want them. You can, of course, buy bricks a hundred or even a dozen at a time, but you're running the risk of breaking a few bricks, your car's springs or your back.

Brick Walls

According to the Brick Institute of America, there are only three kinds of walls you need to be concerned about in building your outdoor structure.

The most common brick wall used in houses is a *veneered* wall. Facing bricks are placed outside the frame of the structure and the brick veneer is attached to the frame by metal ties or by grouting it to wire mesh attached to the studs.

The other type of wall used in houses is a solid masonry *bearing wall*, which means that the

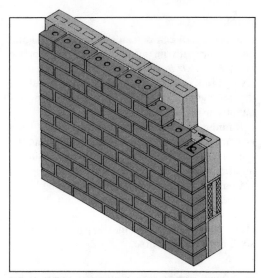

Solid masonry wall. Brick and concrete block provide a structural system.

wall carries the weight of the cap or roof assembly. With this type of wall, there is no frame behind the brick. Instead, the brick, and usually a backup of concrete block or brick, provide both closure and the structural system.

A structure may have a brick *cavity wall* (frequently a bearing wall also). This is a wall in which a space is left between an outer and an inner width of brick. The space is usually filled with insulation. Most often, this type of wall is used when it is desirable to have an exposed brick interior wall. Interior walls of exposed brick, however, can also be built inside veneered or bearing walls.

Veneered wall. Facing brick is placed outside the framework of the structure.

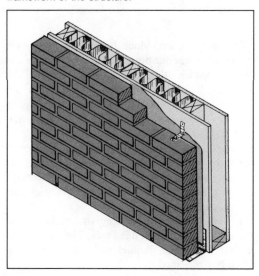

Cavity wall. A space is left between an outer and inner width of brick for insulation.

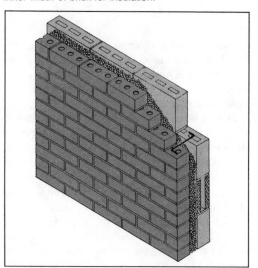

Brick Bonds

Any brick wall can be made more beautiful and interesting with an attractive and appropriate bond. A *brick bond* is the pattern created by laying brick in a certain order. Bonds also add to the strength of the wall. There are five frequently used bonds.

Running bond consists of all *stretchers* (that is, brick laid lengthwise along the wall). Running bond is frequently used in veneered walls and in interior walls.

Common bond is a variation of running bond. It has a course of *headers* (brick laid with the short end along the face of the wall) at regular intervals. These headers may appear every fifth, sixth or seventh course.

Brick Mortar Joints

Mortar joints add to both the beauty and the efficiency of the wall. But their importance is often underestimated. There are six basic types of joints, any of which can change the appearance of a wall. In addition, *striking* the joint properly helps the brick units bond together and helps seal the wall against moisture. "Striking" is the finishing touch given to the mortar in the joint.

Concave joint. Created by using a rounded jointing tool. The joint is rounded, slightly recessed from the face of the brick.

V-Shaped joint. Created with a V-shaped tool, giving a sharper recess from the face of the brick.

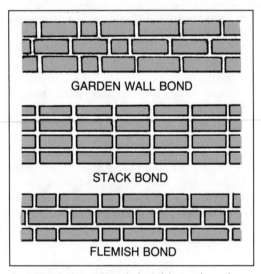

Standard designs of bonds for brick are shown here.

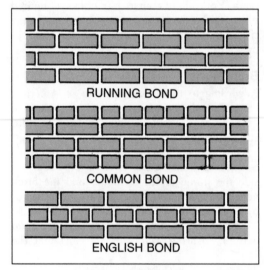

The common and running bonds are the easiest to do.

Flemish bond is often used in Colonial American buildings. Each course is made up of alternate stretchers and headers, with the headers in alternate courses centered over the stretchers above and below.

English bond is composed of alternate courses of headers and stretchers and joints between stretchers in those courses line up vertically.

Stack bond is created by using either all stretchers or all headers and aligning all joints vertically. This bond is used only in veneered or other non-structural walls.

All bonds can be varied by recessing or projecting headers or stretchers to create interesting visual effects. Or you can also use courses of *soldiers* (bricks standing on end) to add variety.

Weathered joint. Made by inclining the joint with the lower edge outward from the face of the bottom brick so that it sheds water readily.

Struck joint. Another inclined joint, but the reverse of the weathered joint; the upper edge of the joint is flush with the face of the top brick with the lower edge recessed.

Rough cut, or flush joint. The simplest joint, made by holding the edge of the trowel flat against the brick and cutting in any direction. The mortar is even with the face of the brick and not recessed.

Raked joint. Made by removing some of the mortar with a square-edged tool. The face of the mortar is flat and parallel with the face of the brick but recessed.

Each of these bonds is about equal in holding strength; the difference is more in their ability to shed moisture or just in the way the make the finished wall look. The most effective in terms of moisture resistance are the Concave, V-Shaped, and Weathered joints.

Brick-Laying Techniques

While you may never develop the skill, finesse and artistry of a professional bricklayer, with a little practice and careful workmanship you can use brick for your outdoor structures with some confidence of structural integrity and aesthetic distinction.

Here are some tips from the Brick Institute of America to help you do this job correctly.

down about 15 minutes before construction begins.

Mix only a small quantity of mortar at a time—about as much as you expect to use within an hour or two. Remember, one bag of ready-to-mix mortar will do about 50 bricks. Your mortar should have the consistency of soft mud; if it begins to stiffen, temper it by mixing in a little water. You may want to rent a powered mortar mixer for larger projects.

The bed of mortar between bricks is called a *joint*. For most projects, allow ⅜ in. between bricks for mortar joints.

To help you keep each course of brick level and straight, use a length of mason's string stretched tightly and level along a line where the

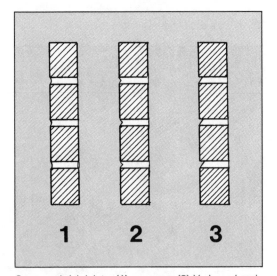

Common brick joints. **(1)** concave, **(2)** V-shaped and **(3)** weathered joint.

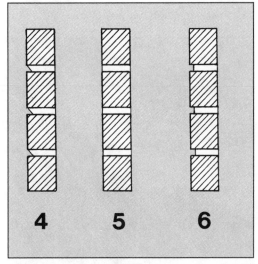

Common brick joints: **(4)** struck joint, **(5)** rough cut or flush joint and **(6)** the raked joint.

It's always a good idea to lay out the first few *courses* (horizontal layers) of brick in a dry run before you actually begin the work. This gives you a chance to recognize possible problems before they develop. This will also tell you if you need to cut any brick or adjust your joint spacing slightly to make a course fit.

Some brick should be laid completely dry; others should be dampened first. To find out which kind you have, draw a circle about the size of a quarter on one of the bricks with a wax pencil or crayon. Use a medicine dropper to put 20 drops of water inside the circle. Wait 90 seconds. If the water is still visible, the brick should be laid dry. If it isn't, the brick should be laid damp (not dripping wet). Hose the brickpile

top edge of each course of brick will be. Be sure to allow ⅜ in. for the mortar between courses.

Bricklayers refer to a *shoved joint* when they want to describe the correct way to lay brick in place. Spread a bed of mortar to a little more than the prescribed thickness (a string line will guide you in this) and roughen the mortar surface by making a shallow furrow with the point of the trowel. Don't try to do this for more than three bricks at a time. Then "butter" one end of a brick with mortar and shove it into the mortar bed with a downward movement so that the top of the brick is level with the string line. When you can do this without moving the brick once it is in place, you will be making professional-type shoved joints. Check the course with a mason's

Use trowel to furrow bed of mortar.

"Butter" the brick and shove it in place.

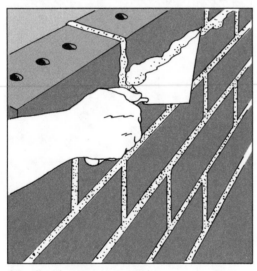

Clip off and reuse excess mortar.

Tool joints for best weather resistance.

level periodically to be sure the bricks are level and plumb. When you shove the brick in place, you'll squeeze out excess mortar at the bottom and end. Use your trowel to scrape off any excess mortar and return it to your mortarboard.

Don't be tempted to lay out the bricks and simply cram the mortar between them. Moisture is the enemy of masonry: unless your job is watertight—and only shoved joints will insure this—trapped water between the bricks will freeze and thaw, eventually destroying your project.

After the bricks have been mortared in place and the mortar is "thumbprint" hard, the joint must be *struck* or tooled to a finish. Use the mason's pointing tool (or short length of ¾-in.

pipe) to strike each joint, working first on the horizontal ones and then on the vertical ones to achieve hard, dense, concave joints.

As you lay the brick, use the edge of the trowel to cut off excess mortar. This can be returned to the mortarboard or simply swept up after the job is finished.

You can cut brick with a broad-bladed chisel. A tap on the chisel with a hammer will score the brick along the line of the cut. Do this on two surfaces of the brick. Then, pointing the chisel inward, strike a sharp blow with the hammer. When a large number of bricks must be cut, you might want to use a power circular saw fitted with a masonry blade or rent a manual cutting machine called a *guillotine*.

BUILDING WITH WOOD

For virtually every outdoor structure you'll build, you will test your skills at both rough and finished carpentry with wood. What follows here is a brief review of the material about carpentry you'll want to read again in Volume 5 of your *Popular Mechanics Do-it-Yourself Encyclopedia* before you begin work on any outdoor structure. You'll also find a short course on joinery in Volume 14.

Horizontal Framing

Horizontal framing of outdoor structures can be as simple as installing fence rails or as complex as a gazebo floor. While fence rails require that the vertical framing or posts be installed first, most outdoor construction requires horizontal framing first.

The *sill plate* is the wood member attached horizontally to the foundation on which the rest of the building sits. Make sure you use a better grade of lumber for the sill and anchor it firmly into the foundation. The most common practice is to install J-bolts (bolts in the shape of a J) in the top of the foundation so the threads begin above sill level. Drill the sills to accept these bolts, then install them with washers and nuts.

Members running horizontally between sills are called *floor joists*. The ends sit on or are notched into the foundation at regular intervals spaced according to how much weight they must carry. If the span or distance between sills is more than 10 or 12 ft., install a girder perpendicular to the joists to support them. You will usually put the girder on piers and short posts.

Install subflooring and flooring over the joists. They are often a single flooring unit for most outdoor structures, usually made from exterior-grade plywood.

Details of vertical framing for larger structures.

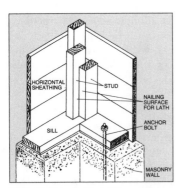

Bolt sill plate to foundation with J-bolts then add vertical framing.

Floor joists are between sill and sole plates in box-sill construction.

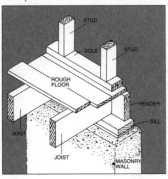

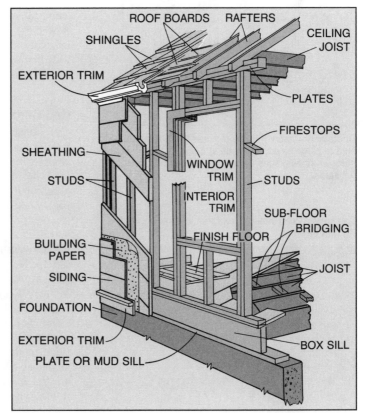

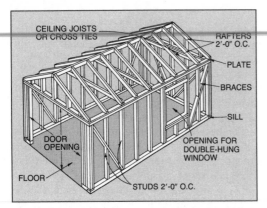

Typical garage framing from sill plate to cap.

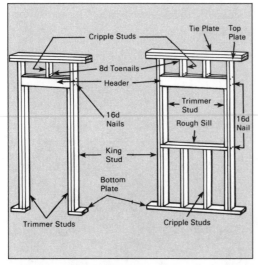

Doors and window framing requires using a header held in place by double studs at the ends with cripple studs in those places where header prevents using full studs.

Cap construction includes roof framing, ceiling, roofing and eaves.

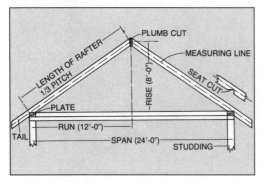

Vertical Framing

Once the outdoor structure has a base, you can begin the vertical framing. Vertical framing or wall framing includes *studs* installed between the *sole plate* and the *top plate*. In fact, the easiest way to install vertical framing is to lay out the sole plate on edge, lay the top plate up against it and, with a tape and square, mark off the location of each stud on the sides of both at the same time. (Typical stud spacing is 16 inches.) Then place the plates on edge about 8 ft. apart on the subfloor, install the studs between them and nail from the plates into the studs. Then lift the wall in place, nail it to the subfloor and vertically brace it until all walls are installed.

For doors, eliminate the sole plate and install a header above the opening. The *header* is a thick member that distributes the load normally handled by the studs and plate it replaces. Double the studs at each side of the door for the header to rest on and install a short frame above the header to span the gap between the doorway and the top plate. Leave openings for windows using the same kind of double studs and headers.

You can overlay vertical framing with exterior siding (single-wall construction) or with plywood and siding (double-wall construction). Where the contents must be kept from freezing in colder climates, install insulation inside the wall before closing it on the inside with wallboard or plywood.

Cap Construction

Cap construction includes installing the roof framing, ceiling, roofing and eaves. Again, the complexity of cap construction depends upon the type, size and use of the outdoor structure. You can build a small storage shed with the ceiling and cap frame in one piece but you need to construct a garage with a full roof frame. If you need to review the procedures for measuring and cutting the compound angles of roof rafters, turn to the information about angles in Volume 1 of your *Popular Mechanics Do-it-Yourself Encyclopedia*.

The horizontal members in roof framing are called *ceiling joists* and they sit atop the walls' top plates. The diagonal members from the roof ridge to the eaves are called *rafters*. Vertical members between the ceiling joists and rafters are *studs* or cripple studs. Spacing between rafters ranges from 16 in. to 36 in., depending on load and local building codes.

Assembling Wood Projects

Because most outdoor wooden projects include large components that are laid out and matched, they are usually easy to assemble. Make sure that plans are nearby because some smaller components may not be perceptively different until measured or assembled. You could end up with a straight-back lounge! Many woodworkers use a basement floor, garage floor or lawn area to spread out components in full view, so that the order in which the components must come together is clear. Often, you assemble the vertical framework first and hold it together by the horizontal framework and then follow up with the non-frame vertical and horizontal members. For a fence, it's the posts, the cross-members, then the boards. Assemble a picnic table the same way: legs held together by cross-framing, then the top and bench.

Metal plates and hangers are used throughout construction.

1. Joist hangers or clips. For dimensional lumber in sizes from 2×4 to 2×14. Holes for nails are punched; the hanger slips over the end of the joist and is fastened to the joist and header.

2. Framing clips. For two- and three-way ties between wall, roof and floor framing. Nail and lag bolt holes are punched.

3. Beam clips (Not Shown) For post-and-beam construction (framing). The clip straddles the post and flush-mounts to the beam. The nail holes are punched and staggered.

4. Truss clips. Teeth for gripping the wood are punched in these flat clips that are used for butt-joining lengths of dimensional lumber, usually 2×4s.

5. Bridge clips. These go between joists and replace the old wooden 1×4 bridging that had to be mitered and toenailed.

6. Base clips. For anchoring 4×4 posts to concrete, these clips are attached to a sill bolt in the concrete.

7. Anchor clips (Not Shown) Used for attaching wood to masonry and concrete surfaces.

8. Storm clips. For fastening trusses or rafters to top plates and stud framing members.

9. Mending plates. Flat steel plates with holes drilled into them for screws. Available in shapes such as Ts, Ls and angled Ls.

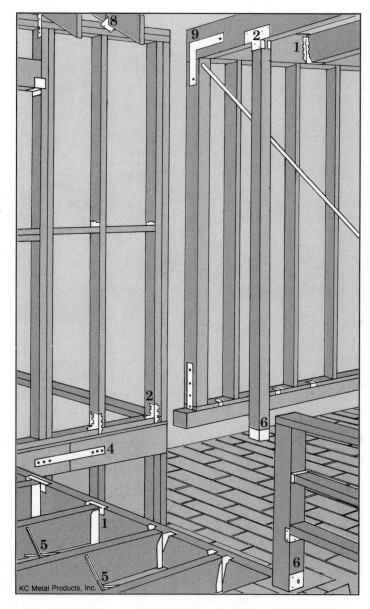
KC Metal Products, Inc.

Fastening Wood

You will, of course, want to have an ample supply of nails, screws and carriage bolts on hand before you begin your project. You will also use finishing hardware in building many outdoor projects: fence gate hinges and latches, storage shed door hinges, deck joist hangers, and reinforcement plates. Their purpose is the same: to fasten two components securely together.

Some of the plans in this book call for metal hangers to reduce the amount of nailing while increasing structural strength. Hangers come in a wide variety. You can chose from joist and beam hangers, framing anchors, rafter anchors, clips, shims, metal bridging, sill plate anchors, utility guard plates, fence brackets, wall bracing, plywood supports, brick veneer anchors, insulation supports, stair brackets, truss plates, post caps and sheer plates.

The combination square can be used for many purposes in constructing outdoor structures.

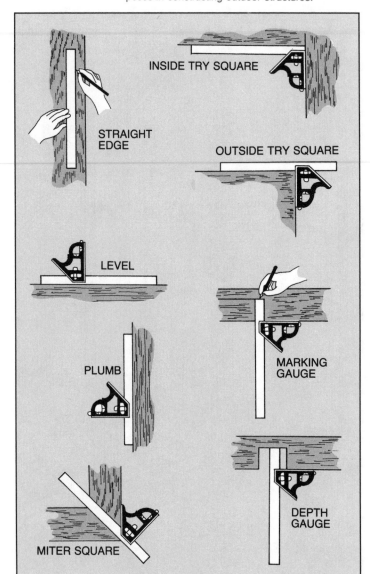

The first step to cutting wood is to measure it.

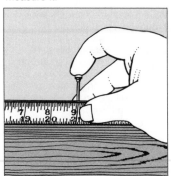

Use the combination square to make sure the mark is straight.

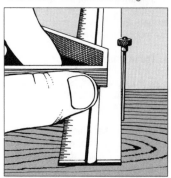

Use the edge of the square to scribe the mark for the cut.

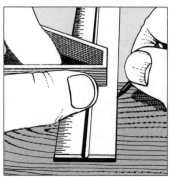

Wood Joints

All outdoor projects can benefit from careful attention to how well the wood joints hold *without* metal fasteners such as nails, screws, bolts or hangers. In fact, the basic skill in woodworking is the art of joining pieces of wood to form tight, strong, well-made joints. Simple joints like the butt, the lap joint and the miter joint are used frequently in rough and finish carpentry for outdoor structures. More complex joints like the rabbet, dado, mortise-and-tenon, slip tenon, box corner and dovetail joints are more commonly used in cabinetry or furniture making.

The two pieces to be joined are called *members*. The steps in joining are first figuring the layout of the joint on the ends, edges or faces of the members, and then cutting the members to the required shapes for joining. Use a combination square, marking gauge and a marker for simple joints while you would use chisels, special saws or routers for more complex joints.

Remember that no joint is any better than the accuracy with which it is cut. To ensure accuracy, make sure the wood stock to be joined is square. If it isn't, mark it again and cut it square before you begin.

The joints used in rough carpentry are often nailed together. You drive nails in a 90° plain butt joint through the one piece and into the end of the abutting piece. You can toenail them at an angle through the faces of both pieces. Studs and joists are usually toenailed to sole plates or sills.

The more complex joints in finish carpentry are usually fastened with glue and you can provide additional strength by dowels, splines, corrugated fasteners, slip feathers, keys and other types of joint fasteners.

Butt Joint

The butt joint is the simplest to make. Use it in rough carpentry and in simple cabinet work such as shelves. The butt joint depends upon metal fasteners for strength.

To make a butt joint you will need a combination or try square, a crosscut saw and a hammer or screwdriver. First, mark lines across the wood surface and edges with the square. Next, cut the lumber with the crosscut saw. Check the cut with the try square and, if it isn't accurate, mark and cut it again. Place the squared end of one member against the square surface of the other. Finally, fasten the members together with nails or screws.

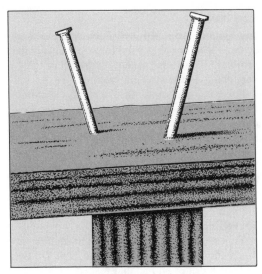

Simple butt joint fastened by toenailing through horizontal member.

Three most commonly used lap joints in rough and finish carpentry.

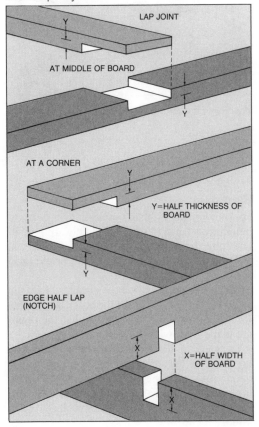

LAP JOINT

AT MIDDLE OF BOARD

Y

Y

AT A CORNER

Y

Y=HALF THICKNESS OF BOARD

Y

EDGE HALF LAP (NOTCH)

X

X=HALF WIDTH OF BOARD

X

Lap Joint

Lap joints are used for door and window screens, outdoor chairs and furniture and similar projects. They are nailed, screwed or glued depending on the strength required.

For a half-lap joint you will need a combination square, knife, marking gauge, back saw, chisel and mallet. First, superimpose one member on the other and mark their width, laying out shoulder lines on edges with the try square. Next, indicate the center line on the edges and end with the marking gauge. Then cut the shoulder of one piece to the center line. Finally, cut the center line to the shoulder and repeat the above steps on the other piece.

You make cross lap, end lap and middle lap joints the same way, joining two centers, two ends or a center and an end respectively.

To mark miter joints with the T-bevel and protractor, adjust the T-bevel to 45° angle with the aid of a protractor. Then place the T-bevel across the edge surface and mark. Draw square lines from either end of the diagonal on the edges. Finally, repeat on the opposite piece of wood.

Make a diagonal cut on the edges with a back saw, following the lines down the face of the board. Repeat on the opposite piece of wood. Finally, check the cuts with the combination square. If they are not accurate, cut them again.

To fasten a miter cut, drive a nail through one piece until it dents the second piece. Pull them apart and spread glue on the cut ends. Rejoin the pieces and completely drive the nail. Finally, drive a nail from the second member into the first.

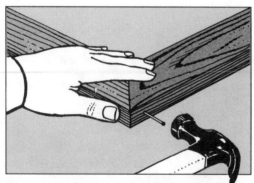

Miter joints are used for trimwork.

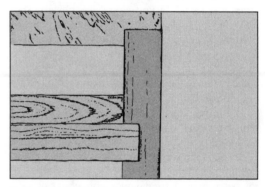

Dado joint strengthens a project.

Miter Joint

The miter joint is also simple and popular in general construction where the joints are visible. The miter joint requires a back saw, hammer, miter box or combination square or T-bevel and protractor.

The miter box is the most popular. Lay the wood in the miter box. Set the miter box saw to 45° and cut. Reverse the angle to cut the opposite piece of wood.

To mark miter joints with a combination square, use the 45° face of the combination square and mark the edges of the wood. Draw square lines from either end of the diagonal on the edges. Then repeat on the opposite piece of wood.

Dado Joint

The dado joint is far stronger than butt or miter joints, especially in joints that must support weight such as fence-posts-to-cross-members and outdoor furniture joints. It doesn't rely on fasteners for strength.

You can make dado joints with either hand tools or power tools. To make a dado joint with hand tools, you'll need a combination square, a saw, a chisel and a marking gauge. First, place the end of one piece across the surface of the other and mark the width. Square the width marks across the surface and edges. Indicate the center of edges between width marks with a marking gauge. Then cut shoulders with a saw to the center line. Remove the wood between the cuts with a chisel or a router plane. Finally, smooth the bottom of the dado, fit the housed piece into the dado and fasten with glue.

Making dado joints with a power tool requires a dado head attached to a radial saw or table saw. Since models are different, it's best to consult the owner's manual that came with your tool.

There are other types of dado joints used in outdoor construction. The stopped dado does not continue across the wood. The stopped housed dado continues across the wood and part of the width of the housed member. The dovetail dado has one shoulder squared and the other at an angle. Each of these require that the housed member is cut or notched to fit.

opposite each other and are drilled vertically. Tools are available to help in marking and installing dowels.

To reinforce a butt joint with dowels, first mark the center of the surfaces to be butted using a marking gauge. Place the surface and end side-by-side and mark the location of dowels on the center lines. Next, bore holes at points designated using a bit of the same diameter as the dowel. Then cut the dowel 1/8 in. shorter than the combined depth of the two holes. Round off the ends of the dowels slightly with sandpaper to ease entry. Place glue in one hole and dip the dowel ends into the glue. Now insert the dowels into the holes and clamp the pieces together for at least 24 hours.

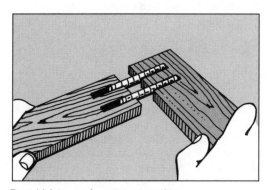

Dowel joints require more carpentry.

Shims are installed between door frame and studs.

Dowel Joints

Doweling is one of the strongest methods of joining wood. Use it in combination with other joints such as butt and miter and as a substitute for mortise-and-tenon in furniture projects. A dowel is a cylindrical piece of wood inserted into a hole and glued. Dowels are usually maple or birch and come from manufactured stock in 3 ft. lengths with a diameter ranging in sixteenths of an inch from 3/16 to 1 in., corresponding to auger bits.

Dowels are smooth, grooved or spiral. Smooth dowels are scored with a file before insertion. Spiral dowels let air and glue rise up their grooves. Make sure that the dowel holes on the corresponding members are located exactly

Finish Carpentry

Finish carpentry for outdoor structures includes covering interior walls, if appropriate, and installing doors, windows, shelves and cabinets.

Self-hung doors come with the door panel hung with hinges on a door frame. You install the frame between the doubled studs and the header. The frame includes side jambs with a door stop, and a head jamb. All you have to do is place the door in the opening, level and align, place wedges between the jambs and surrounding studs, and nail it in place.

Install self-hung windows the same way. Place the window frame in the opening, check for level and plumb, install wedges between jambs and studs, then nail it in place.

Wood Preservatives

Left untreated, wood can rot or become infested by termites and other boring insects. These are the natural enemies of wood that rob it of its strength.

Fungus, mildew and other wood-eating microorganisms need four things to make wood decay or "rot:" oxygen, moisture, the right temperature and, of course, the wood itself. Termites are generally active under the same conditions favorable to decay. They are often attracted to rotting wood. Decay and termite problems can be eliminated by removing any one of the conditions that make them happen.

Pressure-treated wood is tagged by the manufacturer to show compliance with EPA standards. Follow precautions and don't use treated wood in gardens or on any surfaces used for food or as part of play equipment children might put in their mouths.

Pressure-Treated Lumber. Pressure treatment of wood with a preservative has been effectively used for utility poles and railroad ties for many years. Pressure treatment is done by placing dried wood in an airtight cylinder where a vacuum is drawn, sucking air from the wood cells. Then a liquid preservative is pumped into the cylinder under pressure, forcing it deep into the wood. By replacing the oxygen and some of the moisture, the wood looses its attractiveness as a food source to fungus and termites.

Utility poles and railroad ties are usually pressure-treated with oil-based preservatives such as pentachlorophenol or creosote. Creosote leaves an oily residue that makes it inappropriate for outdoor furniture or for use as garden timbers or in planters. Chromated copper

arsenate, or CCA, is a water-based preservative commonly used for pressure treating kiln-dried lumber. It's effectiveness is increased by a chemical bonding to the cellulose compounds within the wood.

There are two levels of preservative treatment used by most commercial suppliers. LP-2 wood is treated to a minimum retention of .25 lb. of preservative per cubic foot of wood. Use LP-2 treated wood for projects that won't come in contact with the ground, such as decking. LP-22 wood has a minimum retention of .40 lb. per cubic foot and this wood *can* make contact with the ground. In fact, LP-22 wood is recommended for most outdoor projects.

CCA pressure-treated wood has gained Environmental Protection Agency approval for use in contact with humans and pets. The only warning offered by the EPA is to not burn any pressure-treated wood because fire separates the chemicals from the wood and the resulting ashes can be harmful.

Paint as a Preservative. Paint, varnish, shellac or brush-on wood preservatives can protect untreated wood for a short time, but they must be applied often to maintain their protection. Maintenance of untreated wood is most important where water collects such as on a patio deck, table surface or in joints. Unfortunately, non-preserving finishes can sometimes *promote* wood decay by trapping moisture under the coating.

Water-Repellent Preservatives. You can apply water-repellent finishes that contain a preservative, a small amount of resin and a very small amount of water repellent. The treatment, which penetrates the wood surface, retards the growth of mildew, prevents water staining of the ends of the boards, reduces warping and protects species that have a low natural resistance to decay. Popular woods such as smooth or rough-sawn western red cedar and redwood will turn a clear, golden tan color.

You can apply the treatment by brushing, dipping or spraying. Liberally treat all lap and butt joints, edges and ends of boards.

One of the preservatives most commonly used by consumers until recently was pentachlorophenol (or *penta*). It has since been suspected by the EPA as unsafe in some applications. It may give off harmful gasses that can be absorbed by breathing or through the skin. There are other wood preservatives that you can apply safely.

PREVENTATIVE PROTECTION

Power tools, both stationary and portable, are indispensable in building any outdoor project. Using power tools, however, creates certain hazards, primarily to your eyes, lungs and ears. Fortunately, protection from wood-chip projectiles, sawdust clouds and screaming routers is easy and inexpensive.

Eye Protection. For eye protection, there are goggles and face shields. Goggles have a pliable rubber frame, plastic lens and elastic strap that hods them snugly over your eyes. The frames are perforated with ventilation holes to deter fogging.

Eye protection, either goggles or face shield, is extremely important to block flying splinters and chips when using a table saw.

A face shield has a flip-down panel that is fitted to an adjustable headband. Face shields are comfortable to wear since no part touches your face but goggles hug the face so they provide better dust protection.

Lung Protection. Nearly all woodworking tools produce fine dust that can irritate your respiratory system. This dust can be filtered out with a dust mask. Essentially a paper filter, the dust mask hugs your face and covers your nose and mouth. Dust masks are available in various styles including disposable types and those that accept replacement filters.

Keep in mind that these masks are designed to handle wood dust only. They will *not* filter out harmful vapors or fumes. In these cases, you must wear a cartridge-type respirator.

Sanding dust can irritate your eyes and respiratory system. Protect yourself by wearing eye protection and a paper dust mask.

Ear Protection. Ear protection is also important, especially in the workshop. The two basic types are the earmuff style and soft-rubber ear plugs. Both styles are effective in reducing harmful noises, but the earmuff style is easier to slip on and off as necessary.

It is a good idea to wear eye protection while using any hand tool, not just power tools. Remember: Owning eye, lung and ear protection is not good enough. You must *use* them every time you work with tools.

Comfortable earmuff-style protection quiets the piercing scream of a router or other power tools. Note that eye protection is also necessary.

CHAPTER 2 Outdoor Furniture Projects

Outdoor furniture provides all the comforts and functions of indoor furniture with the advantages and freedom of being outside. It is sturdier, as functional as it is decorative, and built for rougher use.

In addition to the projects in this chapter, there are more outdoor furniture plans in Volume 16 of your *Popular Mechanics Do-it-Yourself Encyclopedia*. You'll find picnic table and some planter projects in Volume 18.

REDWOOD CHAISE LOUNGE

The redwood chaise lounge is a classic and building one yourself is relatively simple. The inherent characteristics of redwood—impervious to insects and rot—make it the most desirable material for outdoor construction. A lightly

tinted alkyd stain will help retain the attractive color and keep mildew from forming.

You can customize the shape of this lounge to fit yourself or other members of your family. This chaise is designed with a compound curve in the seat. It's this curve that you can modify to take into account individual height and leg length for maximum lounging comfort. The highest point of the curve should be at the back of the knees.

The lounge shown was made with mostly construction-grade redwood. The battens, which make up the seat and back, are clear all-heart grade. The cost of construction-grade redwood is only slightly higher than that of pressure-treated lumber, which has to be painted to cover the unnatural green color resulting from immersion in a chemical bath.

Starting the Lounge

The side panels of this gracefully-styled lounge contain some complex curves, so scale up the dimensions to full size and draw templates of the side panel shapes on a piece of cardboard. The seat shown is shaped to fit a 5-ft., 7-in. person. Cut and test your cardboard template with the person who'll be using the lounge most. Then use the cardboard outline to trace the patterns onto the 2×8×78½-in. boards.

Use a saber saw to shape the side panels, then sand the cuts with a medium grade (100 grit) sandpaper to remove blade marks and round the edges. Work with a sanding block and smooth out the rough spots made on the curves while sawing.

Cut a 1¾-in. radius at each corner of the two 2×4×28-in. backrest pieces. At the same time, cut 1¾-in. radius at the corners of the two 1×4×15½-in. support pieces.

Use a 1⅛-in. spade bit to bore three holes in the backrest pieces, one at each end and one at the center (as shown on the drawing). Also bore holes at both ends of the support pieces.

Materials List Chaise Lounge

Key	Pcs	Size and description (use)
A	48	1½×¾×23½" redwood lumber (seat slats)
B	2	2×8×78½" redwood lumber (side panels)
C	3	2×4×20½" redwood lumber (side panel spacers)
D	2	2×4×28" redwood lumber (backrest supports)
E	2	1×4×15½" redwood lumber (support pieces)
F	2	7⅛" dia. redwood circles (wheels)
G	1	1⅛" dia.×20½" birch dowel (backrest top)
H	1	1⅛" dia.×22" birch dowel (backrest pivot)
I	1	1⅛" dia.×23½" birch dowel (backrest adjustment)
J	1	1⅛" dia.×28" birch dowel (axle)
L	2	2×4×14" redwood lumber (leg pieces)
M	2	¼"×4" birch dowel (wheel dowel pins)

Fasteners

14	3½" galvanized exterior screws
100	1¼" - 1⅝" galvanized exterior screws

Redwood and cedar split easily. Drill pilot holes for nails and screws. Round all edges.

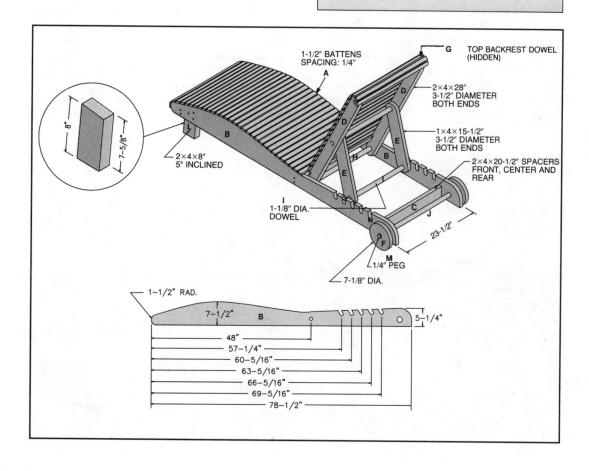

At the same time, bore the side panels for the dowels, the 7⅛-in.-dia. redwood wheels for the axles, and the holes for the backrest pivots. Also bore holes that form the bottom of the adjustment slots for the backrest. The hole for the backrest is blind. Bore from the inside of the side panels, penetrating about ¾ inch. Measuring from the front edge of the side panel, bore the backrest dowel hole 48 in. o.c. and 2⅛ in. from the bottom edge.

The on-center measurements for the five slot holes are shown in the drawing. The hole for the wheel dowel is 74⅞ in. from the front edge of the side panel and 1⅝ in. from the bottom edge.

Use a protractor to set a bevel rule and mark two angles for the backrest adjustment slots, drawing down from the top edge to the tangent of the five holes. Mark the front angle (the side toward the front of the chaise) at 10°. Mark the back angle at 5°. With a handsaw, carefully cut down to the holes along the angle lines.

Assemble the frame for the backrest. Locate the 1⅛×22-in. dowel at the bottom of the rest and put it in the blind holes on the side panels. The dowel for the center hole of the backrest carries the support ends. As you slip this dowel into place, add the two supports. Complete the backrest frame by installing the 20½-in. dowel.

In the remaining holes in the supports, install the 23½-in. dowel, leaving an equal extension on the outer side of each support. Then, with a ⅛-in. bit, bore holes through the redwood and into the dowels.

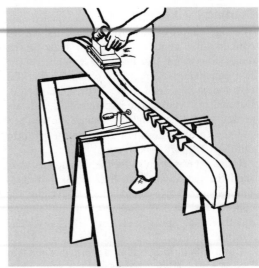

Clamp two panels together so shapes will be identical as you adjust the shape of side panels.

Fit the lower backrest dowel into the holes bored for it in the side panels. Assemble the side panel frame using 20½-in. 2×4 spacers as shown in the drawing. The front spacer is angled 10° toward the rear of the lounge and positioned 2½ in. from the front. The center spacer is positioned ahead of the backrest dowel. The rear spacer is located ahead of the wheel dowel. From the back, bore holes from the outside of the side panels and into the spacers and secure with two galvanized screws, recessing the heads slightly.

Dowels at base of backrest are mated with holes in side panels when seat frame is assembled.

Attach spreader between side panels for extra support at the adjustable backrest.

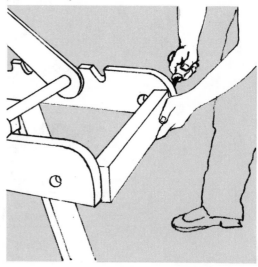

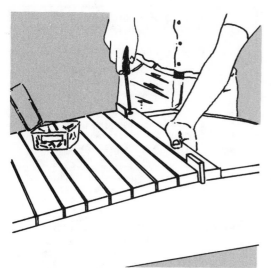

Use spacer block to evenly space the clear redwood slats about ¼-in. apart.

Cut a 10°-angle at the bottom of each 14-in. 2×4 leg piece. Use galvanized screws to attach them to the backside of the front spacer. Align with the angle of the spacer so the angled cut of the leg stands flat. Insert the 28-in. dowel through the holes at the rear of the side panels and bore ¼-in. holes through each end at a point ½ in. from the end. Fit on the 7-in. redwood wheels and drive 4-in.-long ¼-in. dowel pins through the holes to hold the wheels on the axles.

Applying the Redwood Slats

How you position the slats is a critical factor in making the backrest adjustment work right. Set the backrest at the first upright adjustment. Measure up ¼ in. from the top of the side panel and mark as the starting point for the slats.

Attach the slats to the backrest by boring ³⁄₁₆-in.-dia. holes and securing with 1⅝-in. galvanized screws, one screw at each end of a slat. Cut the slats ¾×1½×23½-in. They overhang the back 1½ in. on each side. Space the slats ¼ in. and wrap two slats around the radius at the top.

Again position the backrest upright and measure ¼ in. forward from the lower slat on the backrest and mark as the starting point for seat slats. Space and secure these in the same manner.

Finally, cut a slat 20½-in. long and fit it from the outside edge to the outside edge ¼ in. below the lowest slat on the backrest. This will fill in much of the space when the backrest is fully reclined, without creating an annoying gap.

Redwood comes finish sanded four sides with corners rounded. All that's necessary before applying an alkyd base sealer is light, touchup sanding.

Since this chaise lounge is relatively simple and economical, you can mass produce two or four for your deck or pool. You can add colorful cushions, if you choose, or use them just the way they are.

Short slat at bottom of backrest fills space between slats on backrest and those on the seat.

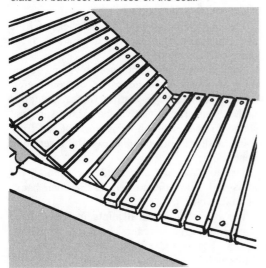

Insert a ¼-in.-dia. dowel in the axle to keep the wheels from working their way off.

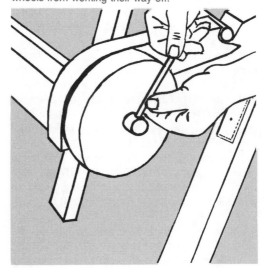

Materials List
Settee

Key	Pcs	Size and description (use)
A	2	2×4×22″ lumber (arm)
B	2	2×3×22⅛″ lumber (back leg)
C	2	2×3×22¾″ lumber (front leg)
D	2	2×4×22″ lumber (side frame)
E	4	2×3×18″ lumber (chair back)
F	2	2×4×55″ lumber (front and back frame)
G	2	2×4×18″ lumber (frame brace)
H	6	2×4×17″ lumber (back slat)
I	4	2×2×18″ lumber (seat cleat)
J	6	1×6×17″ lumber (seat slat)
K	2	2×2×9″ lumber (front table leg)
L	2	2×2×11½″ lumber (rear table leg)
M	6	2×4×18″ lumber (table slat)
N	2	2×2×21¼″ lumber (table cleat)
O	1	2×4×21″ lumber (umbrella support)

Fasteners

	8	⁵⁄₁₆″× 4″ lag screw with flat washer
	6	⁵⁄₁₆″× 3½″ carriage bolt with nut and flat washer
	2	⁵⁄₁₆″× 4″ carriage bolt with nut and flat washer
	12	⁵⁄₁₆″× 3″ lag screw with flat washer

Miscellaneous

Cushions to suit
8d galvanized nails
6d galvanized finishing nails
½″ diameter dowels

SETTEE

Attractive, comfortable and easy-to-build describe this redwood settee.

This project is designed to accommodate standard outdoor cushions, available from catalogs and home centers. In addition, if you want to be protected from the rays of the sun, you can add a matching umbrella.

Use straight, construction-grade redwood or cedar. These weather-resistant woods will give you years of service. Both woods splinter very easily so it is necessary to drill pilot holes for all nails and round all edges.

The settee calls for 2×3s and 2×2s which may not be available in your area. If you can't find them, rip 2×4s to the proper width. A 2×3 is 1½×2½-in. and a 2×2 is 1½-in. square. Smooth out the cut edges on a jointer or portable power plane.

A motorized miter box or radial-arm saw is the preferred tool for cutting the project parts. Check these tools to insure they are cutting accurately before you begin this project. Use a sharp plywood blade to minimize wood splintering and sanding.

Begin construction by cutting out the frame components. These include the side frames (**D**), front and back frame (**F**), frame braces (**G**) and seat cleats (**I**). Check the actual thickness of these parts to make sure they are 1½-in. thick. If they are not, then you will have to make allowances in the table's width.

Now, cut the arms (**A**), table slats (**M**), table cleats (**N**), seat slats (**J**), back slats (**H**) and table legs (**K, L**) to length. If you are going to add an umbrella, cut the umbrella support (**O**) to length as well.

Set the motorized miter box to cut the 68° angle in the front and rear legs (**C, B**). Cut the angle in a scrap piece of material and trace this angle onto the workpiece to use as a guide for positioning the blade. Make the cuts in all four legs. If you work with long lumber stock, you will need to make only one cut because the waste already has the 68° angle.

Pay careful attention to each leg's different top angles (see drawing). Again, cut scrap to use as a template in laying out the workpieces for cutting. Cut the legs, and mark them so that you know the correct position for assembly.

Finally, cut the 5° angle on each of the chair backs and tops of the table legs.

Lay out the notches in the table legs and the arm contours for cutting. Use a band saw to cut these parts to shape.

Sand all the parts for assembly, and round over all edges with sandpaper. If you prefer, round over the edges with a router, equipped with a ¼-in. rounding over bit. Make sure you round over the top showing edge of the front frame with a ¾-in. rounding over bit inserted in your router.

Use a stationary disc sander to smooth the arms and round the corners of the chair backs and table cleats.

For assembly, dowel all joints, including those which will have fasteners, with one ½-in.-dia. dowel. For added strength you can glue the joints with a waterproof adhesive.

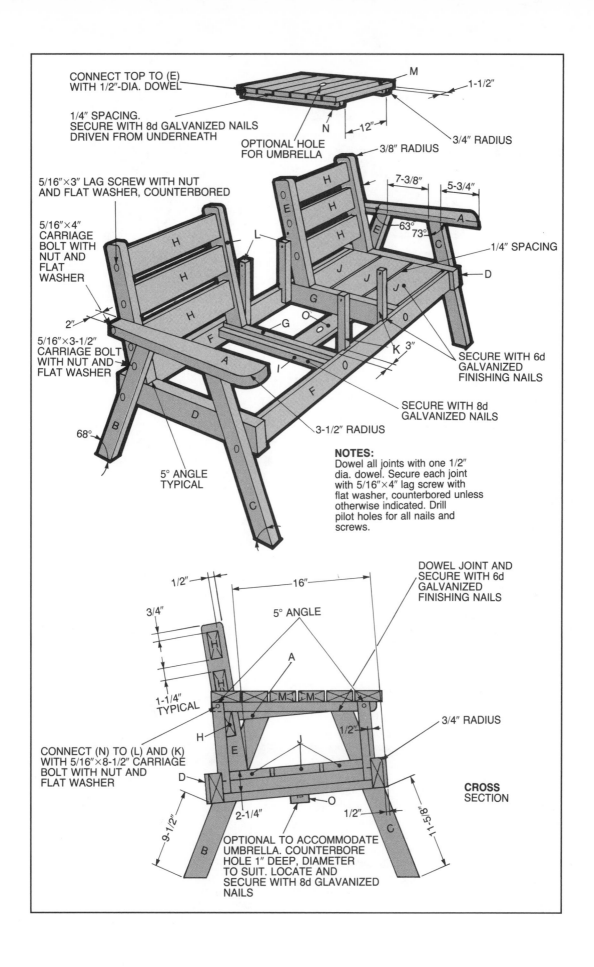

CONNECT TOP TO (E) WITH 1/2"-DIA. DOWEL

1/4" SPACING. SECURE WITH 8d GALVANIZED NAILS DRIVEN FROM UNDERNEATH

OPTIONAL HOLE FOR UMBRELLA

M

1-1/2"

N

12"

3/4" RADIUS

3/8" RADIUS

7-3/8"

5-3/4"

5/16"×3" LAG SCREW WITH NUT AND FLAT WASHER, COUNTERBORED

5/16"×4" CARRIAGE BOLT WITH NUT AND FLAT WASHER

A

63°

73°

1/4" SPACING

D

2"

5/16"×3-1/2" CARRIAGE BOLT WITH NUT AND FLAT WASHER

68°

5° ANGLE TYPICAL

3-1/2" RADIUS

K 3"

SECURE WITH 6d GALVANIZED FINISHING NAILS

SECURE WITH 8d GALVANIZED NAILS

NOTES:
Dowel all joints with one 1/2" dia. dowel. Secure each joint with 5/16"×4" lag screw with flat washer, counterbored unless otherwise indicated. Drill pilot holes for all nails and screws.

DOWEL JOINT AND SECURE WITH 6d GALVANIZED FINISHING NAILS

1/2"

16"

3/4"

5° ANGLE

A

1-1/4" TYPICAL

H

3/4" RADIUS

CONNECT (N) TO (L) AND (K) WITH 5/16"×8-1/2" CARRIAGE BOLT WITH NUT AND FLAT WASHER

H

E

D

J

1/2"

CROSS SECTION

9-1/2"

2-1/4"

1/2"

11-5/8"

B

C

O

OPTIONAL TO ACCOMMODATE UMBRELLA. COUNTERBORE HOLE 1" DEEP, DIAMETER TO SUIT. LOCATE AND SECURE WITH 8d GLAVANIZED NAILS

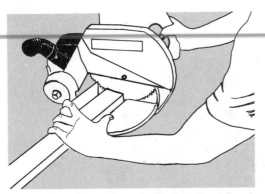

Cut all miters on a motorized miter box. Use mitered wood scrap to draw cutting lines.

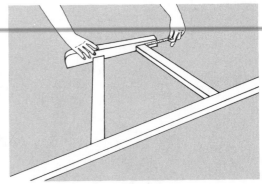

Carefully align sides for assembly. Use a board as straightedge to keep leg bottoms straight.

Keep in mind that all carriage bolt heads should show on the assembly. You should also cut off and file smooth any bolt portion that projects beyond the washer and nut.

Assemble the side frame to the front and back frame with dowels and 8d galvanized nails driven partially in. Install the frame braces with $5/16 \times 4$-in. lag screws and flat washers. Drill all fastener holes and counterbore so the screw heads are flush with the wood's surface. Don't overtighten.

If you have never counterbored holes, you must counterbore first, with an appropriate sized spade bit or Forstner bit, and then drill the pilot hole.

Position each arm and leg assembly on a flat surface. Once they are positioned correctly, dowel the joints. Install the dowel (one per joint) and drive two 6d finishing nails at each joint. Drive these nails from underneath.

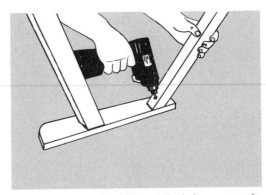

Attach legs to arm by drilling a pilot hole on an angle then securing with wood screws.

Measure the proper position where the frame will contact each leg set. Then attach one leg set to the frame. First, remove the nails temporarily driven in one end of the frame and position the leg set. Mark the fastener positions, and drill counterbores and pilot holes. Secure the leg set to the frame with $5/16 \times 4$-in. lag screws and flat washers.

Follow this same procedure for installing the remaining leg set.

Now, locate the chair backs. Drill for and install dowels to join the chair backs to the frame. Also mark the fastener locations in the two outside chair backs, and drill and counterbore where indicated in the drawing. Again, mark them so each can be installed later in its proper position.

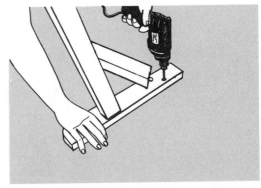

Locate and drill dowel holes for each joint. Use a Forstner bit for a flat-bottomed hole.

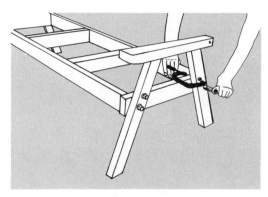

Counterbore and drill fastener holes and assemble sides to frame. Clamp holds cross piece for assembly.

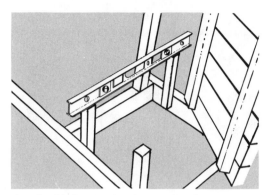

Attach table legs, and make sure they form a level plane for the table installation.

Test-fit back upright assembly to be sure bottom angles give correct slope.

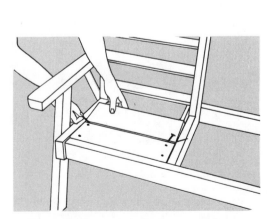

Install seat cleats and then the seat slats with nails or screws. Use nail heads to space slats.

Install the back slats to the chair backs with $5/16 \times 3$-in. lag screws and flat washers, counterbored. Carefully align each piece or the back will not be flat. Poor alignment will create a problem at installation.

Set the assembled backs in position, and insert the $5/16 \times 4$-in. carriage bolt through each arm into the chair back. Do not secure at this time.

Attach the four table legs onto the frame with 6d galvanized nails. Then install the spaced table slats to the table cleats with 8d galvanized nails. Drive the nails into the cleat surface to hide the nails. Drill the appropriate size hole for the umbrella stem at this time. Place the assembled top onto the table legs. Mark the fastener locations and the dowel locations where the back table slat adjoins the chair back. Drill the dowel and fastener holes.

Next, install the table onto the legs. You will have to remove one of the chair backs so you can insert the table with the dowels in place. Secure the table to the legs with $5/16 \times 3\frac{1}{2}$-in. carriage bolts and flat washers. Secure the backs to the leg sets.

If you plan on adding an umbrella, counterbore a hole into the umbrella support. Then insert the umbrella stem through the table's hole while positioning the umbrella support under the frame. Once the umbrella stem is vertical, mark the umbrella support's position. Secure the support with 8d galvanized nails.

Finish the assembly by attaching the seat cleats and seat slats with the appropriate size fasteners. Space the seat slats $\frac{1}{4}$ in. apart.

Finish sand rough spots, and apply an appropriate wood preservative.

Key	Pcs	Size and description (use)
A	9	2×6×72″ lumber (top and seats)
B	2	2×4×26½″ lumber (table support)
C	2	2×4×60″ lumber (seat support)
D	2	2×4×34⅞″ lumber (leg)
E	2	2×4×26½″ lumber (table cleat)
F	2	2×4×31¼″ lumber (brace)

Materials List
Picnic Table

Fasterners

	16	5/16″×3½″ carriage bolt with nut and flat washer
	40	5/16″×4″ lag screw with flat washer
	5	5/16″×2″ screw with flat washer

PICNIC TABLE

There are few experiences that are as exhilarating as dining in the great outdoors. Whether at the cabin or in your own back yard, this redwood picnic table will accommodate you and five other diners.

Select lumber that is weather-resistant. Woods like redwood and cedar are ideal. Also make sure all of the lumber is straight and free of loose knots.

Begin construction by cutting the table supports (**B**) and seat supports (**C**) to length. Then cut the 1½×1½-in. bevels in these workpieces as shown in Detail 1. Cut these out with a saber saw equipped with a long fine-tooth saw blade. If you encounter too much wood splintering, mark the cutting line with a sharp utility knife and cut up to the line.

A motorized miter box is ideal for cutting the angles required on the legs (**D**) and braces (**F**). Set this tool to cut a 60° angle. Then cut a scrap piece of material to use as a template for laying out the legs for cutting. Cut the legs to size.

Next, saw the 59° angle at one end of each leg brace. Afterwards, use a protractor to lay out

the 31° angle at the remaining end. Cut this acute angle on a band saw or with a saber saw.

Cut the table cleat (**E**) to length, and make the ¾-in. bevel on the miter box.

Sand all parts for assembly, including the tops (**A**) and seats (**A**). Round over all showing edges with sander or router.

Lay out the sides for assembly. Place the table support, legs and seat support on a flat surface. Use a straightedge to insure the legs are on a straight line. Position the materials to suit the locations specified in the drawing. From this point, the easiest way to proceed is to drive two 2½-in. screws into each joint. Then remove one screw, and drill a 5/16-in.-dia. hole for the fastener. Install a 5/16-in. carriage bolt with nut and flat washer. Continue removing screws, drilling pilot holes and installing carriage bolts.

When the side is assembled, use the section as a template for positioning the remaining side. Again, use the same technique for side assembly.

Place the five 2×6s which form the top on a flat surface. Set two or more pads underneath to keep the lumber off the ground. Then space the

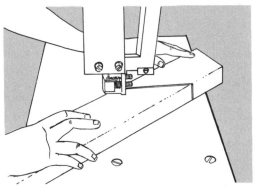

Lay out the 31° angle on the brace and cut with band saw. Use a ½-in. blade.

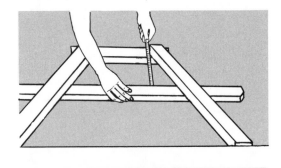

Carefully position the side for assembly. Use a board as straightedge to keep leg bottoms aligned.

Complete the picnic table by applying a wood preservative. Be sure the preservative is safe for use on these surfaces; food you intend to eat could pick up toxic substances. Carefully read the manufacturer's directions to be sure the preservative is non-toxic.

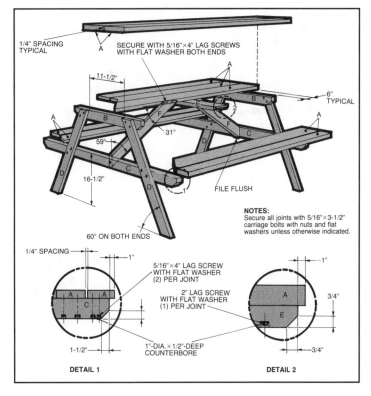

1/4" SPACING TYPICAL

SECURE WITH 5/16"×4" LAG SCREWS WITH FLAT WASHER BOTH ENDS

11-1/2"

6" TYPICAL

31°

59°

16-1/2"

FILE FLUSH

60° ON BOTH ENDS

NOTES:
Secure all joints with 5/16"×3-1/2" carriage bolts with nuts and flat washers unless otherwise indicated.

1/4" SPACING

5/16"×4" LAG SCREW WITH FLAT WASHER (2) PER JOINT

2" LAG SCREW WITH FLAT WASHER (1) PER JOINT

1"-DIA.×1/2"-DEEP COUNTERBORE

1-1/2"

3/4"

3/4"

DETAIL 1   **DETAIL 2**

top workpieces ¼ in. apart. Position the table cleat, and mark the fastener hole positions (one per joint). First counterbore the locations, and then drill the holes to accommodate the fasteners. Finally, secure the table cleat with $5/16 \times 2$-in. lag screws and flat washers.

Now, position one brace to the top, and mark to locate the fastener. Drill the hole, and attach the brace with a $5/16 \times 4$-in. lag screw and flat washer. Install the remaining brace the same way.

Place one side assembly in position up against the brace. Square the assembly and mark its location. Also, mark the section for drilling. Counterbore and drill the fastener holes. Then install the side with $5/16 \times 4$-in. lag screws and flat washers. Attach the remaining side assembly.

With the aid of another person, turn the unit upright. Position the seats, and mark the seat supports for drilling. Counterbore and drill the fastener locations, and secure the seats, spaced ¼ in. apart, with the same size 4-in. lag screws and flat washers.

Square off the seats and top with a carpenter's square, and cut them flush with a circular saw. Use a plywood blade.

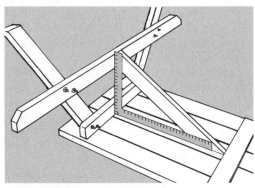

Assemble table cleat and brace to top first. Then square and attach each side assembly.

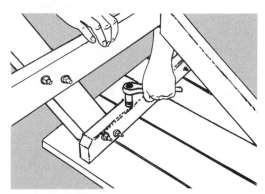

Attach top boards to support braces. Use socket wrench to tighten bolts on legs.

3 Outdoor Play Equipment

Popular play equipment includes such children's favorites as the play center, sandbox and playhouse. This chapter shows you how to build these outdoor projects. Other projects for children's play equipment you can build are in Volume 18 of your *Popular Mechanics Do-it-Yourself Encyclopedia*.

BACKYARD PLAY CENTER

Commonplace backyard swingsets often lose appeal to youngsters and become little more than unattractive obstacles to mowing the lawn. A stimulating play environment is valuable for growing children. It increases motor skills, builds muscles, and improves cardiovascular strength.

If you want to provide your youngsters with a backyard play center that will be used, the secret is visual excitement. It must have features galore so childen can easily switch from one activity to another to keep their interest level high.

This activity center has swings, balance beam, seesaw, climbing ladders, monkey bars and a raised platform. It also can include a sandbox you can build now or add later.

The design of the play center is modular; the balance beam, swings and monkey bars, platform, seesaw and sandbox are all separate projects you can build as time and your budget permit. Each new module added will rejuvenate your youngster's interest in the center.

Use construction-grade redwood for the project. Redwood has a natural resistance to insects and decay and most of it is mill-sanded with smooth, well-rounded edges so there are no splinters to catch small fingers. More important, redwood does not expose young children to the toxic chemicals used in pressure-treated lumber.

Use 4×4s for principal load-bearing components. If you're building the center for older, larger children you may want to substitute 4×6s across the top.

Backyard play structure provides creative activity.

Where to Start

Since the play center measures 25 ft. from one end to the other, you'll have to be sure you have ample space for it in your yard, or modify the plans before you begin to suit the space you do have. After you have carefully studied the plans and instructions here, saw each piece listed and stack identical pieces together because they are likely to be used together.

After all pieces have been cut you can start on the assembly. Begin at the balance beam end. That's the easiest part, but it does require sinking a 4×4 post at least 18 in. deep in the ground.

While you have the post hole digger in hand, dig *two* 18-in.-deep holes 25 ft. apart. One hole is for the support post of the balance beam at one end of the play center. The other hole is for the support post of the seesaw that will be at the other end of the play center.

Use a 4×4, 40 in. long for the support post for the balance beam. Notch it at the top to accept the width and thickness of a 2×6. Measure and mark the notch 1½×5½-in. at the top end of the post. If you have a bandsaw, use it to cut the notch. If your only saw is a circular saw, make several cuts, working toward the end of the post. Then use a wood chisel to clear away the waste.

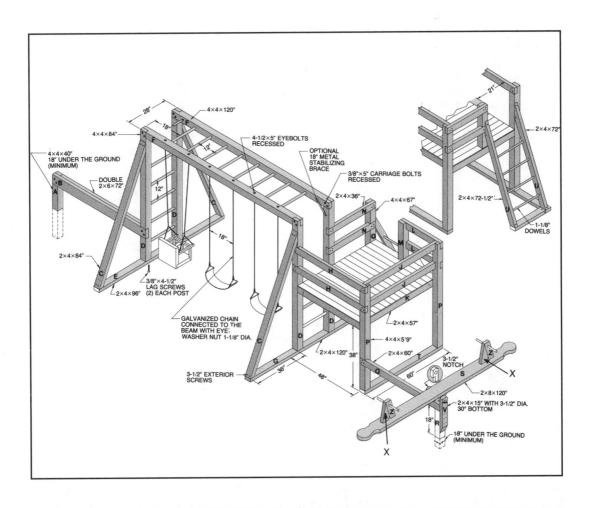

Materials List
Backyard Play Center

Key	Pcs	Size and description (use)
A	1	4×4×40" redwood (balance beam post)
B	1	2×6×72⅜" redwood (balance beam)
	1	2×6×65⅜" redwood (balance beam)
C	3	2×4×84" redwood (side supports)
D	4	4×4×84" redwood (ladder stiles)
E	1	2×4×96" redwood (ground support)
F	2	4×4×120" redwood (monkey bar stiles)
G	1	2×4×120" redwood (ground support)
H	2	2×4×55" redwood (left-side guard rails)
I	2	2×4×48" redwood (platform frame)
J	2	2×4×57" redwood (seesaw-side guard rails)
K	4	2×4×57" redwood (platform frame)
L	1	2×4×30½" redwood (ladder-side guard rail)
	1	2×4×29" redwood (ladder-side guard rail)
M	1	4×4×25" redwood (short support post)

Fasteners

	14	⅜"×½" roundhead carriage bolts
	30	⅜" flat washers
	30	⅜" lock washers
	30	⅜" nuts
	14	⅜"×4½" to 6" lag screws
	125	3" galvanized exterior screws
	2 lb.	No. 8 ring shank, galvanized nails (splitless)
	46	8d aluminum finish nails

Key	Pcs	Size and description (use)
N	2	2×4×35½" redwood (monkey bar-side guard rails)
O	1	4×4×67" redwood (platform post)
P	2	4×4×67" redwood (platform post)
Q	1	2×4×60" redwood (seesaw fulcrum bar)
R	1	4×4×40" redwood (seesaw support post)
S	1	2×8×120" redwood (seesaw)
T	1	2×4×60" redwood (platform ground support)
U	2	2×4×62½" redwood (platform ladder stiles)
V	1	2×4×15" redwood (seesaw pivot support)
W	1	4×4×7" redwood (seesaw pivot support)
X	2	2×4×12" redwood (seesaw handle sections)
Z	2	2×4×14½" redwood (seesaw handle sections)
	16	1×4×48" redwood (platform decking)
	1	1⅛" dia.×11" dowel (seesaw fulcrum pivot)
	4	1⅛" dia.×22½" dowels (slanted ladder rungs)
	2	1⅛" dia.×24" dowels (platform ladder rungs)
	5	1⅛" dia.×24" dowels (monkey bar ladder rungs)
	8	1⅛" dia.×24" dowels (monkey bars)

Miscellaneous

Baby swing, sling swings, redwood deck stain, thinner, brushes, 80 and 100 grit sandpaper

Join the long and short parts of the balance beam. Use No. 8 deck screws 3½-in. long to join the 65⅜-in. piece to the 72⅜-in.-long 2×6. Off-set the ends by 3½ inches. One end of the assembly mates with the notch cut in the balance beam. The other end will fit a notch cut into the stile of the climbing ladder.

Building the Climbing Ladder

Two 84-in.-long 4×4 posts form the stiles of one of the ladders in the play center. In one post, cut a notch to fit a 2×6, locating the top of the notch 20¾ in. from the base. Cut this notch on the outside of the 4×4. At the inside of the top end, cut a notch to fit half the thickness of a 4×4. Make a similar notch in the top of a second 84-in.-long 4×4. These notches mate with the horizontal 4×4s which form stiles for the monkey bars.

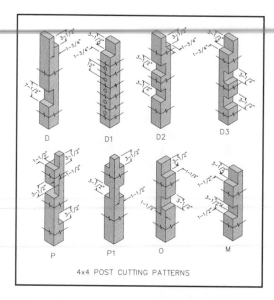

4x4 POST CUTTING PATTERNS

To make well-fitting notches, make several saw cuts starting with the width of the notch.

Knock away the remaining wood with blows from a hammer, breaking off the pieces.

Smooth the notched surface by using a sharp chisel to cut away all of the rough surfaces.

Now assemble the ladder. Remembering that the notch for the balance beam is at the outside of the 4×4, bore 4 holes 1½ in. deep and 12 in. o.c. at the center of the inside of this 4×4. The lowest hole is 12 in. from the lower end. Use a 1⅛-in. spade bit for this. (You can also use an expansion bit and brace.) Bore matching holes in the inside face of the second 4×4 (on the side with the notch at the top end).

Fit 1⅛×24-in. birch dowels into each of the four holes, then mate the other ends with the holes in the second 4×4, making certain that the dowel ends are firmly seated into each 4×4. Bar clamps tightened across the 4×4s ensure that the dowels are seated and the width is even.

Use a ⅛-in. drill bit to bore pilot holes through the 4×4s and into the end of each dowel. Take care in this operation, since you will be boring only about ¾ in. from the edge of the 4×4. As each hole is completed, pound in an 8d aluminum nail.

Position a 2×4, 96 in. long against the lower end of the completed ladder. The legs of the ladder should be 34 in. from each end of the 2×4. Bore two pilot holes and secure the 2×4 to the ladder ends with ⅜×3½-in. galvanized deck screws. Then join the support post for the balance beam to the opposite end and lower the 40-in. post into the hole you dug in the ground.

Use a level on the balance beam to adjust the depth of the hole, then backfill the hole. You can use soil to backfill, or fill the hole with concrete. If you use concrete, be sure the post is perpendicular to the ground before the concrete sets.

Fit an 84-in. 2×4 between the end of the ground support and one stile of the ladder. Mark the ends at 22½° and 67½°. Check that the 2×4 will fit from the end of the ground support to a point about 7 in. from the top of the ladder stile. Saw the bevels and secure the brace with No. 8×3½-in. galvanized deck screws. Repeat this step for the opposite side of the ladder.

Notch a 67-in. long 4×4 at one end to accept a 2×4 and make a second similar notch 8¾ in. below. Lay the ladder and this post on the ground and attach a 120-in.-long 2×4, locating the first leg of the ladder 34 in. from the end to align it with the leg of the climbing ladder. Locate the post 26 in. from the opposite end of the 120-in. 2×4. This leaves 28½ in. between the ladder and the post. Bore ³⁄₁₆-in. pilot holes and secure the ladder and the post to the 2×4 using ⅜×4½-in. lag screws.

Monkey Bars

Notch the ends of two 120-in. long 4×4s to mate with the notches in the two ladder stiles. Starting 18 in. from one end, mark and then bore 1⅛-in. holes 12-in. o.c. and 1½-in. deep on the inside of each 4×4. The last hole should be 18 in. from the end.

Countersink holes at major joints so that washers and nuts will be recessed out of harm's way.

View of balance beam showing how it is fitted to support post and ladder stile.

Use a spacer block when nailing deck boards.   A ¼-in. to ⅜-in space is desired.

Building the Platform End

With the balance beam of the play center completed, begin assembling the platform end. Use two 84-in. long 4×4s to form the uprights of the ladder which supports the other end of the monkey bars. Notch them at the top the same way you did the ladder stiles. Cut these notches on the inside of the supports. Saw a 1½×3½-in. notch to fit a 2×4 on the outside of the left leg 17 in. from the top. Make the same size notch at the same location, but on the platform side of the second leg (see drawing). Make a second notch below each of these, starting 8¾ in. from the bottom of the first notch. Use these notches for the guard rails which surround the platform.

Bore 1⅛-in.-dia. holes for three rungs in these legs, as you did in making the climbing ladder, starting 12 in. from the bottom. Insert 24-in. dowels for ladder rungs, bore pilot holes, and secure with aluminum nails.

Insert 1⅛×24-in. dowels and secure them in place by drilling ⅛-in. pilot holes and nailing with 8d aluminum nails.

Next, lay out the ⅜-in.-dia. holes for eye bolts from which the swings will be suspended. These holes are bored in the horizontal leg of the monkey bars which aligns with the balance beam. The first hole is 17 in. from the end. The second hole is 18-in. on center from the first. From this point bore four more holes, spacing 18 in. between the pairs with 16 in. space between each of the two holes. Countersink so washers and bolts will be recessed to eliminate the possibility of a youngsters snagging their clothing or scratching themselves. Then, bore the ⅜-in.-dia. holes for the eye bolts. Install the 3¾-in. eye bolts, flat washers, lock washers, and nuts and tighten firmly with a socket wrench.

Mate one end of the monkey bars with the climbing ladder, then raise the ladder for the other end into position.

Make sure the ladder and the monkey bars fit together firmly. Then bore two holes through opposite corners of the notches for 3½-in.-long roundhead carriage bolts. Start the hole on the outside, using a 1⅛-in. spade bit, countersinking the hole ½-in. deep to recess the flat washer, lock washer and nut. Then bore the hole through with a ⅜-in. bit.

Secure joint with bolts, washers and nuts, tightening with a 9/16-in. socket wrench. Repeat this procedure for the three remaining joints. Position a 2×4 brace from the end of the ground support to the top of the ladder, as you did on the balance beam end. The braces at each end should align, with the ground support extending farther outward on the opposite side.

Building the Platform

Build the 4×5-ft. platform next. Its framing components are two 2×4s, 48 in. long and four 2×4s 57 in. long. The 57-in. 2×4s butt against the two 48-in. pieces, spanning their length at 16-in. centers. Use deck screws to construct the frame. Make sure the frame is square, then lay down sixteen 1×4 boards spaced about ¼ to ⅜ in. apart.

Nail boards down with 8d box head, ring shank galvanized splitless nails. Splitless nails are thin and less likely to cause the redwood platform boards to split. Ring shanks will keep the nails from popping as the play center is used and the wood ages.

Two additional 4×4s, 67 in. long support the platform. Notch these corner posts to accept guard rails. The post aligned with the swing support must be notched for the seesaw support as well.

Cut a notch 3½×1½-in. deep on the inside top of each corner post to fit a 2×4 guard rail. Then, notch the outside edge to accept a second guard rail. Make identical notches 8¾ in. down from the bottom edge of the completed notches.

If you plan to add the seesaw now, notch the post which aligns with the swings. Cut the notch to fit a 2×4, locating it 14 in. up from the bottom end (see drawing). Align these posts with the ends of the 60-in. platform. Use a 60-in. 2×4 as a ground support pad, and attach it with lag screws to the bottom ends of the two posts, one post at each end of the 2×4.

Notch a 31-in. long 4×4 to accept two 2×4 guard rails on the outside. Cut one notch at the top and the second 8¾ in. below. The bottom of this posts rests on the deck.

Temporarily tack the platform in position against the swingset posts, 38 in. from the bottom edge of the ground support. Align it with the outer edges of the outside swingset post and the free-standing post. Tack to all three posts. Position the outside corner posts flush with the 48-in. sides of the platform and temporarily tack the platform at the same height. Temporary tacking allows some post movement as you fit and secure the guard rails.

Use two 55 in. long 2×4s for the guard rails on the left of the far side of the platform from the ladder. Secure these with 3-in. No. 8 galvanized deck screws. Two 2×4s measuring 57 in. long form the guard rails on the seesaw side of the platform. These butt against the faces of the guard rails already installed and at the other corner post. Position and secure these two guard rails using galvanized deck screws.

Install the two 36-in.-long 2×4s between the leg of the swingset and the platform corner post. Secure with galvanized deck screws. With guard rails complete, secure the platform between them, using No. 8 deck screws 3½ in. long.

Position the short post on the edge of the platform at a point 22½ in. from the swingset side. Tack this to the platform, then position the two 30-in. 2×4 guard rails and secure them with deck screws. After this, secure the post to the platform with 4-in. lag screws.

Platform Ladder

Construct the ladder from two 62½-in. 2×4s. Cut the ends at 24° at the bottom and 66° at the top.

To make the ladder, bore four 1⅛-in.-dia. holes 1 inch deep in the sides of each piece. Start 12 in. from the bottom (24° angle end) and space them 12 in. apart. Use 1⅛×22¾-in. dowels for ladder rungs.

Press the dowels firmly into the bored holes, clamp the assembly together, then bore holes from the backside of the ladder into the dowels using a 1/16-in. drill bit. Drive an aluminum nail into each hole as it is made. Finally, attach a 22¾-in. 2×4 to the left foot of the ladder using No. 8×3½-in. deck screws. Place the ladder so that this ground pad butts the end of the ground pad supporting the right platform posts. Join the two with deck screws driven in at an angle. To complete the platform assembly, attach the top of the ladder to the guard rail posts using deck screws.

A 1⅛-in.-dia. dowel is attached with deck screws to the balance point of the seesaw 2×8.

Detail of seesaw fulcrum assembly showing how pieces fit.

Use a compass to draw the radius of the seat shape.

Saw the shape with a saber saw, keeping blade outside line.

Smooth the cuts with wood rasp and a sanding block.

Attach seesaw handle to the board with galvanized deck screws.

Constructing the Seesaw Support

Build the support for the seesaw first. It consists of a 60-in. 2×4 and a 40-in. 4×4 post. Notch the top of the post to fit the 2×4 and join with roundhead carriage bolts the same way you secured the monkey bars to the two ladders. Lower the post into a hole 25 ft. from the balance beam support post hole. Fit the other end of the 2×4 into the notch on the vertical platform support. Secure with bolts. Then backfill the hole making sure the post is perpendicular. You can also set this post in concrete.

Eight inches from the outside edge of the post, notch the 2×4 1¼-in. deep by 3½-in. to fit a 4×4. Using a 7-in. piece of 4×4, cut a 2¼-in. notch to fit the thickness of the 2×4. With a saber saw, cut the top to a 3½-in. diameter and bore a 1⅛-in. hole centered approximately one inch from the top of the 4×4, cutting 1½ in. deep. Mate the notches in the 4×4 and 2×4 and join them with deck screws. Cut a 45° taper on a 15-in. piece of 2×4. Cut the same radius and bore the same size hole at the same location as on the 4×4. Don't attach the 2×4 to the outside of the post yet.

Building the Seesaw

The seesaw board is a knot-free 2×8, 120-in. long. Use a saber saw to cut two radiuses at each end (see drawing) and to shape the seat.

Assemble the handle sections. Make these from two 2×4 pieces, one 12-in. and the other 14½-in. Bore a 1⅛-in. hole through the 12-in. pieces, centering it 1 in. from the end. Cut 35° angles on the bottom and 55° at the top of the 14½-in. pieces. Join the 55° angle to the top end of the 12-in. 2×4, using deck screws. Locate these assemblies 14 in. from the ends of the seesaw board, bore holes from the underside of the board and secure with three deck screws in each assembly. Press 12-in. dowels through the holes, centering them, then bore pilot holes.

Find the balance point of the seesaw and mark it. Position an 11-in. piece of 1⅛-in. dowel at the balance point and bore four holes through the dowel and into the board and secure it firmly using deck screws. Fit one end of the dowel through the hole in the 4×4 support attached to the seesaw support and fit on the 15-in. 2×4. Hold the dowel parallel with the support and attach the 15-in. piece to the support post.

Open covers on sandbox form a
bench or play surface.

Closed covers keep out neighborhood cats and other wildlife.

SANDBOX

Resembling an oversize carpenter's tool box,
the covers of this sandbox keep the sand clean
and dry and provide protection from neighborhood pets when the box is not being used. When
opened, this unique design provides two large
benches or tabletop play surfaces.

Start by cutting the two 42-in. 2×12s and two
39-in. 2×12s for the sides. Assemble them into a
42-in. square box. Check for squareness by
making sure the corner to corner diagonals are
equal lengths. Hold the box square by tacking a
temporary batten across the bottom of the
2×12s.

Build the two covers. The lids are oversize
(42×45½-in. overall). This extra width of each
lid is needed so the hinges won't bind. The
rabbetted 2×4 ends add strength to the seats.

Fabricate the hinges as shown on the drawing
and fasten. Hold the bracket in place with a
clamp while you verify the swing of the lid to be
sure it won't bind. Then glue and screw it in
place.

Finally construct the handle/leg pieces. Cut
these pieces to size and dry assemble to check
the fit. Then attach them with glue and screws.

One-third of a yard of sand will further stabilize the sandbox and keep it in place. Be careful
about the kind of sand you buy for the sandbox.
Very white sand is often made up of particles of
coral that could scratch young fingers. Builder's
sand often contains toxic impurities that should
be kept away from youngsters who may be
tempted to taste their culinary sand creations.
Most home centers will stock sand made especially for sandbox use.

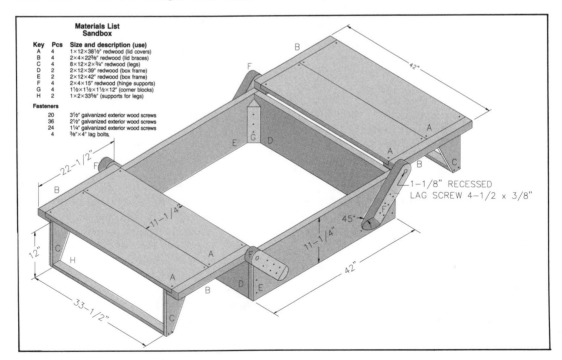

Materials List
Sandbox

Key	Pcs	Size and description (use)
A	4	1×12×38½" redwood (lid covers)
B	4	2×4×22⅜" redwood (lid braces)
C	4	8×12×2×¾" redwood (legs)
D	2	2×12×39" redwood (box frame)
E	2	2×12×42" redwood (box frame)
F	4	2×4×15" redwood (hinge supports)
G	4	1½×1½×1½×12" (corner blocks)
H	2	1×2×33⅝" (supports for legs)

Fasteners

	20	3½" galvanized exterior wood screws
	36	2½" galvanized exterior wood screws
	24	1¼" galvanized exterior wood screws
	4	⅜"×4" lag bolts

42"

1-1/8" RECESSED
LAG SCREW 4-1/2 x 3/8"

22-1/2"

11-1/4"

45°

11-1/4"

12"

42"

33-1/2"

PLAYHOUSE

In the mind of a child, a small shed becomes Buckingham Palace, an Alaskan cabin or a space ship—all in the same day! Even the most basic playhouse can be transformed into something wonderful by a child's imagination. The playhouse shown here is easy to construct with common materials. When your child outgrows it, you can use it as a storage shed.

With all materials on site, you can build this playhouse in a weekend or a week of summer evenings.

The first step in constructing this playhouse is to determine its exact location on your lot. Cut one 4×6 skid to 84 in. and the other two 90 in. long. Arrange the two longer skids beneath the door location for step support. Position them with the top of the skid flush with ground level. Use stakes, lines and level to aid accurate installation of these footer skids.

Framing detail for a playhouse. When your children have outgrown their use of it, you can reclaim it as a storage shed.

	Materials List	
	Playhouse	

Key	Pcs	Size and description (use)
A	3	4×6×96″ lumber (skids)
B	8	4×4×96″ lumber (posts)
C	6	2×6×144″ lumber (floor joists)
D	2	2×6×120″ lumber (lower frame, sills)
E	4	2×4×120″ lumber (rafters)
F	8	2×4×72″ lumber (rafter supports)
G	9	2×2×72″ lumber (subframe, doorstop)
H	3	1×6×120″ lumber (ridge, fascia)
J	13	1×6×72″ lumber (floor boards)
K	5	48×96×½″ exterior plywood
L	3	48×96×½″ sheathing plywood

Fasteners:
'8d, 10d, 12d, and 16d galvanized nails
1″ galvanized roofing nails

Miscellaneous:
2	6 ft. galvanized eave drips
3	Galvanized butt hinges
65	sq. ft. shingles and roofing felt

Tools:
Circular or crosscut saw, hammer, square, screwdriver, carpenter's tape, and stakes, line and level for laying out the foundation

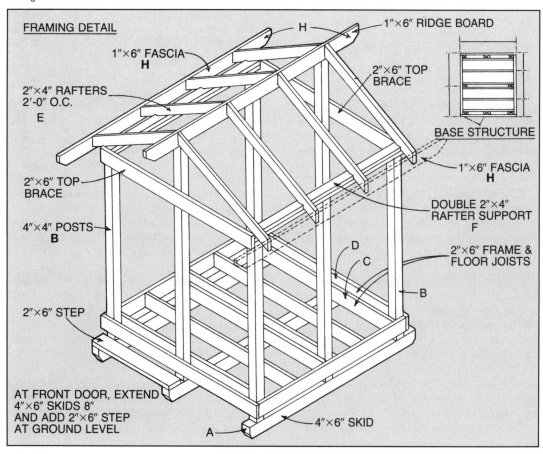

FRAMING DETAIL

1″×6″ RIDGE BOARD

1″×6″ FASCIA — H

2″×4″ RAFTERS 2'-0″ O.C. — E

2″×6″ TOP BRACE

BASE STRUCTURE

1″×6″ FASCIA H

2″×6″ TOP BRACE

DOUBLE 2″×4″ RAFTER SUPPORT F

4″×4″ POSTS B

2″×6″ FRAME & FLOOR JOISTS

D
C
B

2″×6″ STEP

AT FRONT DOOR, EXTEND 4″×6″ SKIDS 8″ AND ADD 2″×6″ STEP AT GROUND LEVEL

A

4″×6″ SKID

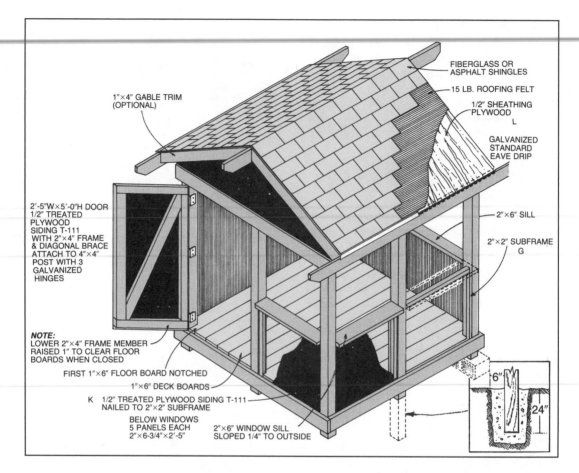

1"×4" GABLE TRIM
(OPTIONAL)

FIBERGLASS OR
ASPHALT SHINGLES

15 LB. ROOFING FELT

1/2" SHEATHING
PLYWOOD
L

GALVANIZED
STANDARD
EAVE DRIP

2'-5"W×5'-0"H DOOR
1/2" TREATED
PLYWOOD
SIDING T-111
WITH 2"×4" FRAME
& DIAGONAL BRACE
ATTACH TO 4"×4"
POST WITH 3
GALVANIZED
HINGES

2"×6" SILL

2"×2" SUBFRAME
G

NOTE:
LOWER 2"×4" FRAME MEMBER
RAISED 1" TO CLEAR FLOOR
BOARDS WHEN CLOSED

FIRST 1"×6" FLOOR BOARD NOTCHED

1"×6" DECK BOARDS

K   1/2" TREATED PLYWOOD SIDING T-111
NAILED TO 2"×2" SUBFRAME

BELOW WINDOWS
5 PANELS EACH
2"×6-3/4"×2'-5"

2"×6" WINDOW SILL
SLOPED 1/4" TO OUTSIDE

6"

24"

Now cut six of the 4×4 posts to 75 in. long. Using 16d nails, toenail three each to the outside skids. Use the square to set the posts true vertical. Then toenail the two 4×4×96-in. center posts to the center skid, following the plan.

Stabilize the posts by attaching the double 2×4 rafter supports to the tops of the 75-in. posts. Use four of the 2×4×72-in. pieces. Attach them with 12d nails and construction adhesive, checking to make sure they are square and level.

From each 10-ft.-long 2×6, cut a piece 75 in. long; the pieces left over will become two of the 30¾-in. window sills. Cut one 2×6×72-in. piece and two more window sills from one of the 144-in.-long pieces. From another 2×6×144-in. piece, cut one piece 72 in. long and use the remainder for one window sill and the front step.

Attach two 2×6×72-in. pieces to three 4×4 posts on each side. The bottom edge of the 2×6 should be 3 in. above the 4×6 skid. Use 12d nails and construction adhesive.

Now complete the lower perimeter frame by attaching two 2×6×75-in. pieces at front and rear using 12d nails and construction adhesive. Make sure the entire frame remains level and square. The outside dimension of the lower 2×6 frame should be 75 in. on a side.

Cut the remaining three 2×6×144-in. piece in half for the six floor joists. Refer to the plan for placement. Attach the joists to posts and frame using 10d nails and construction adhesive.

Build the 2×2 subframe to receive ½-in. treated plywood siding and window sills. Recess the subframe 1 in. from the exterior side of the 4×4 posts. Attach the 2×2 material to the 4×4 posts using 10d nails and construction adhesive. Finished subframe height at the windows should be 2 ft., 5 in. above the top of floor joists.

Next, cut 1×6×120-in. material to 104 inches. Trim the ends according to the plan, if desired. Use 8d nails to toe-nail the 1×6 ridge board atop the 4×4 center posts.

Referring to the plan, cut eight 2×4 rafters from the 10 ft. lengths. Toenail the rafters in place 24-in. o.c. (on center) using 10d nails. End rafters should be flush with the ends of the rafter support.

Attach 1×6 fascia to rafter ends using 8d nails and construction adhesive.

Install 1×6×72-in. floor boards to 2×6 joists using 8d nails and construction adhesive. Cut notches to fit around the 4×4 posts where needed. Floor board ends should be flush with the outside edge of the 2×2 subframe.

Now cut treated plywood siding panels to fit between the 4×4 posts. Attach to the subframe using 8d nails and construction adhesive.

Install the roof with the 6 in. overhang front and rear. Use 8d nails to attach ½-in. sheathing plywood to the rafters. Sheathing should just cover the top edge of the 1×6 fascia boards. Add a layer of roofing felt. Attach galvanized eave drips to the ends of the sheathing plywood using 8d nails. Install shingles with roofing nails.

Hang the door on the 4×4 corner posts using 3 galvanized hinges with screws. Close the door to locate the position of a 2×2 door stop on the 4×4 post opposite the hinges.

Attach 2×6 window sills to the 2×2 subframe using 10d nails and construction adhesive. Slope each sill ¼ in. to the outside for drainage.

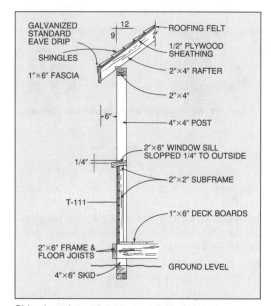

Side view shows finishing detail for the playhouse. With modifications in basic dimensions and finishing details (as shown below), you can give your playhouse a customized, personal touch to match your carpentry skills and the imagination of your youngster.

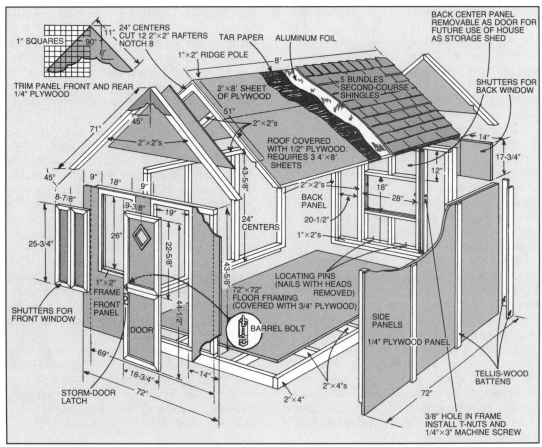

Fence and Gate Designs

You can construct a fence easily with basic building materials: wood, fasteners and finish. Yet each fence can have its own purpose and personality. The material in this chapter adds important information and projects to the section about fences in Volume 9 of the *Popular Mechanics Do-it-Yourself Encyclopedia.*

The first thing to do after you have decided to build a fence is to check your local zoning regulations and building codes. Most areas have rules about fence heights, property line setbacks and aesthetics. Check your property deed as well because some include restrictions and reservations that may affect your fence plan.

Once you've checked zoning, review your boundary survey. If you don't have an up-to-date survey of your property's boundaries, consider having it done before you begin installing a permanent structure. A few dollars spent on a survey can save much embarrassment and possible legal problems. To allow for survey errors, plan to install the fence several inches inside the boundary. Discuss the plan with your neighbors. They may share the cost of installing and maintaining a fence directly on the property line because it adds to the value of their home as well. When you've reached agreement, remember to confirm it in writing so there are no misunderstandings—now or later.

Good fence planning also includes checking for the location of utility lines and water pipes. Your survey should show the locations of utility easements, paths that underground utilities can use to reach your home and others within the neighborhood.

Make sure you also clear debris away from your property line before beginning. Tear out any old fencing and post footings, clear out interfering trees or shrubs, and move large rocks that may make the job more difficult later. These preliminary efforts will make the actual construction go faster later.

Fence Materials

The selection of materials is as important as the design. Good materials can double the life of your fence and dramatically reduce the cost over the life of the fence. After you have chosen the style of the fence you want to build, the next step is to estimate how much lumber or other materials you will need.

To estimate materials, first draw a simple sketch of your yard on a piece of graph paper (available at drug and stationery stores). Draw the location of your planned fence or fences. Then use another sheet of graph paper to draw a typical section of your fence using a scale of ½ inch to 1 foot. Other than for rail and chain link fences, make sure each fence section is 8 ft. wide or less so you can use standard dimensional lumber. Determine what parts you need to build one fence section and multiply it by the number of sections you will construct. List wood and hardware components separately.

Setting Posts

Once you've designed your fence and selected materials, begin construction by setting the posts. Posts are generally one-third longer than the above-ground height. For example, a 6-ft.-high fence should be built with 8-ft. posts. Dig holes one-third the height of the post above ground plus six inches. For example, a post for a 6-ft. fence goes 2 ft., 6 in. into the ground. Of course, much depends upon the weight of above-ground materials, the size of the posts, and local frost conditions. Posts that are not set deeper than the frost line will be lifted by the expansion of freezing ground water, damaging the fence.

Dig the post hole two to three times wider than the post; a 4×4-in. post is installed in a hole 8 to 12 in. wide. If you have only a few posts to install, a manual post-hole digger will do the job. If, however, you are installing many post holes, you may want to rent a power-driven earth auger.

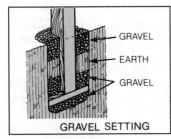

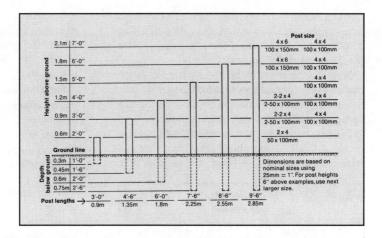

Setting fence posts with gravel and earth. Bottom cross member offers additional support.

Typical fence post size and depth.

Finished fence is attractive to you and to your neighbors.

Materials List
Vertical Board Fence

Pcs	Size and description (use)
1	4×4×96″ fence post
1	2×10×96″ top rail
1	2×6×96″ bottom rail
16	1×6×72″ boards
1	1×4×96″ top rail trim

Fasteners:
Galvanized 30d and 6d nails

Tools:
Shovel, posthole digger or auger, level and a hammer

Vertical Board Fence

The easiest large fence to build is the vertical board fence. With minor modifications, it can be a wind break, a privacy fence, or a semi-private fence.

First, dig post holes 8 ft. apart o.c., 30 in. deep and 12 in. across. Lay about 6 in. of gravel in the bottom of the hole and set the post so that the bottom is 24 in. below ground. You'll want to be sure, however, that it's set below the frost line in your area. Mix cement and pour it around the post in layers, tamping it down periodically to remove trapped air. Use a carpenter's level to check plumb on two sides of the post, then hold the post in place with an anchored support board. Make sure you crown the cement so water will run away from the post.

Once the concrete around the posts has hardened, install the top and bottom rails using two 30d galvanized nails for each post. Tack one end

in place, then use a level to verify position before finishing the nailing. You can install the top rail trim either before or after you install the top rail.

Next, install the fence boards making sure they are level. Space each board ¾ in. apart by placing one board edgewise between the boards as you put them up. You can vary this spacing. Install them with 6d galvanized nails carefully placed in an even horizontal row across the fence.

Slat Fence

A similar design, called the *slat fence*, offers additional privacy with ease of construction. It is more closed than the vertical board fence, while offering a decorative design from either side. It is popular for shared-cost property line fences.

The first step in constructing a slat fence is to determine the exact position of posts using stakes, line and level. Then dig the post holes approximately 36 in. deep. Measure 42 in. from one end of the 4×6 posts and draw a line on both sides of the wide dimension. Nail 2×4 blocking pieces to the post using 12d nails, making sure the 2×4 end is on the line.

Next set the posts in the holes 6 ft., 3½ in. on center using concrete, compacted gravel or soil. Stabilize the posts by nailing on the 2×6 top cap using 12d nails and construction adhesive.

Pre-assemble the top support, nailing two 2×4s to the 2×6 top plate, allowing space between them for a 1×6 fence board. Use 12d

nails. Partially assemble the bottom support nailing only one 2×4 in position with 12d nails. Install the bottom support assembly (with only one of two lower 2×4 supports in place) by nailing to the 2×4 blocking material.

Next, toenail the upper support assembly into place. Make sure the top edge of the upper assembly is between 75 and 77 in. above the bottom edge of the lower support. This allows room enough for the 6-ft. boards to fit between the upper and lower supports.

Insert the fence boards between the upper 2×4 supports and against the single 2×4 lower support. Space 12 boards evenly within the 6-ft. span. Nail the boards into place ½ in. apart along the lower 2×4 support using 6d nails. Once all 12 boards are in place, nail the second 2×4 lower support into place using 12d nails.

Now run a bead of construction adhesive down the length of the 6-ft. 1×4 center supports and position them along the center line of the fence boards. Toenail the ends of the 1×4 supports into the 4×6 posts using 6d nails.

Simply repeat this process to build the additional fence sections.

Materials List — Slat Fence

Key	Pcs	Size and description (use)
A	2	4×6×120" fence post
B	5	2×6×72" top, bottom plate, supports
C	1	2×6×72+" top cap (continuous)
D	2	2×4×72" lower supports
E	12	1×6×72" boards
F	2	1×4×72" center supports

Fasteners: Galvanized 6d and 12d nails, construction adhesive

Tools: Circular or crosscut saw, post hole digger, hammer, square and carpenter's rule or tape

Plans for a slat fence with a gate.

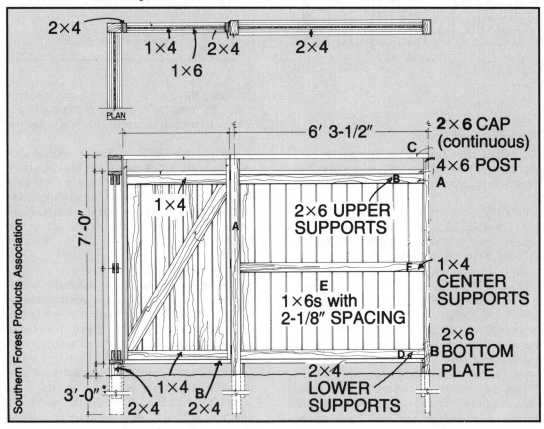

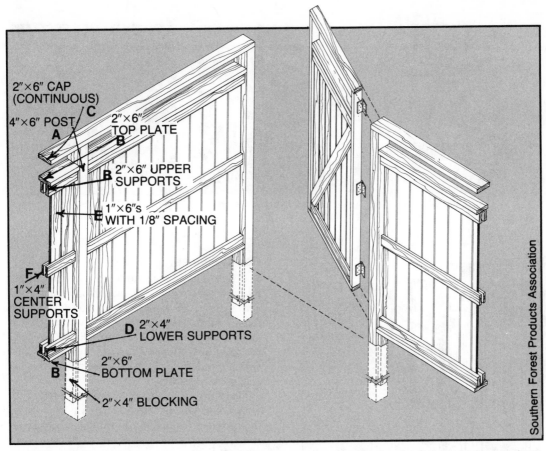

2"×6" CAP (CONTINUOUS)

4"×6" POST

A
C
B

2"×6" TOP PLATE

B 2"×6" UPPER SUPPORTS

E 1"×6"s WITH 1/8" SPACING

F 1"×4" CENTER SUPPORTS

D 2"×4" LOWER SUPPORTS

B 2"×6" BOTTOM PLATE

2"×4" BLOCKING

Southern Forest Products Association

Construction details for a slat fence and gate.

Wooden Gate

The gate shown goes with this slat fence, but it can be modified easily to fit nearly any board fence design.

First, build a 2×4 frame using 12d nails. Attach two pieces 44 in. long to the top and bottom of two vertical members 75 in. long. Install both 1×4 bottom supports to the frame using 12d nails. Be sure to leave a space between them about one fence board wide.

Next, partially assemble the upper support, nailing only one 1×4 in the proper position with 12d nails. Insert fence boards into the bottom support (between the 1×4s), spacing the 7 fence boards evenly across the span. Nail them into place along the upper 1×4 with 6d nails. Once all the boards are in position, nail the second 1×4 upper support in place with 12d nails.

Carefully trim the remaining 1×6 for use as a diagonal brace. You should have a flush fit between the 1×4 supports and the 2×4 frame members. Nail the brace into place using 6d nails.

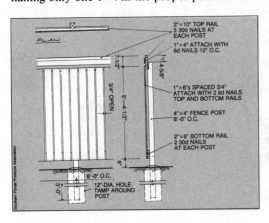

PLAN

2"×10" TOP RAIL
3 30d NAILS AT EACH POST

1"×4" ATTACH WITH 6d NAILS 12" O.C.

7-1/2

1-4/5/8"

1"×6"s SPACED 3/4" ATTACH WITH 2 6d NAILS TOP AND BOTTOM RAILS

3/4" OPEN

5'-4-1/2"

4"×4" FENCE POST 8'-0" O.C.

2"×6" BOTTOM RAIL 2 30d NAILS AT EACH POST

6"

8'-0" O.C.

3'-0"

12"-DIA. HOLE TAMP AROUND POST

Southern Forest Products Association

| Materials List |
| Wooden Gate |

Pcs **Size and description (use)**

Pcs	Size and description (use)
2	2×4×96" frame components
1	2×4×144" frame components
4	1×4×48" upper and lower supports
8	1×6×72" boards

Fasteners:
Galvanized 6d and 12d nails, construction adhesive
1½" and 3" galvanized or stainless steel wood screws

Tools:
Circular or crosscut saw, post hole digger, hammer, square, and carpenter's rule or tape

Digging holes for fence posts is easier with power auger.

Auger lifts dirt, depositing it where it can be used to refill.

Post is held in position with layers of gravel and cement.

Some fences must follow the terrain in steps. Bottoms of boards are trimmed to match the slope of the terrain while the top of the boards are trimmed to be level in each section.

Board Fences

For back yard privacy, nothing beats a tall board fence. It's also easy to build with basic materials and skills. The board fence, however, does require more design time since it will become a major component of back yard living. A well designed board fence can make outdoor rooms within your yard; a poor design becomes a distractive eyesore.

There are many ways to include interest to your board fence. One popular way to reduce the boxed-in feeling of a board fence is to open some viewing areas that are not critical to privacy. For example, you can leave boards off a section or two to open a view to a large tree or shrubbery letting the view through the open section provide the privacy. Separate the boards slightly to let some breeze come through. You can also break the vertical lines of a tall fence with horizontal patterns such as battens, lattice, rails or even alternate designs from top to bottom.

Run string between corner posts to align posts.

Measure each post for the proper spacing of stringers.

Cripples are attached to posts for attaching the stringers.

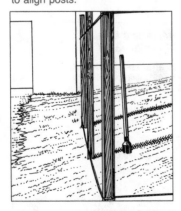

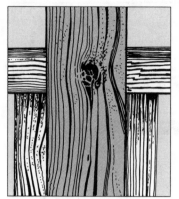

Stringers are easily installed on both sides of a post using cripples.

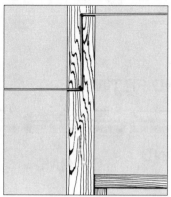

Run string to outline top of fence, adjusting for terrain.

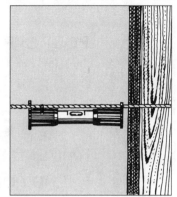

Line level on string ensures the top of fence will be level.

Break up blank fence surface area by using planters, planter shelves, trellis, lighting brackets or alternate designs at regular intervals.

Another design option is to reflect the exterior design of your home as much as possible with your fence. Use horizontal siding, textured paneling or other house siding for fence boards. This is especially effective when the fence abuts the house.

You can also use non-wood materials for boards: fiberglass sheets, acrylic plastic, canvas or mica sheets.

Board fences are simple to construct. Build a sturdy post and rail frame and then attach the boards. Dimensions vary around the standard 6-ft. boards hung on 2×4 rails between 4×4 posts installed 6 to 8 ft. apart. Longer fence runs should have added support or shortened rail spans to make them sturdier. You can also add support by cross-fencing, a third rail, enlarged post footings or bracings.

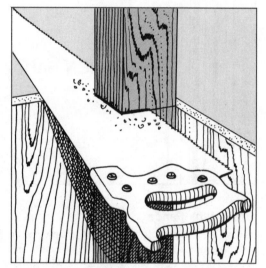

Top of posts can be cut off flush with the fence top once the boards are installed.

Slight drop in terrain can be accommodated by using longer posts. Note that stringers are level.

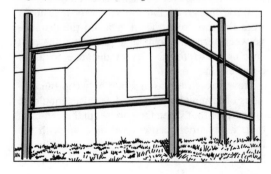

Install boards on frame, making sure each board touches but does not move the top string.

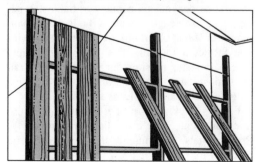

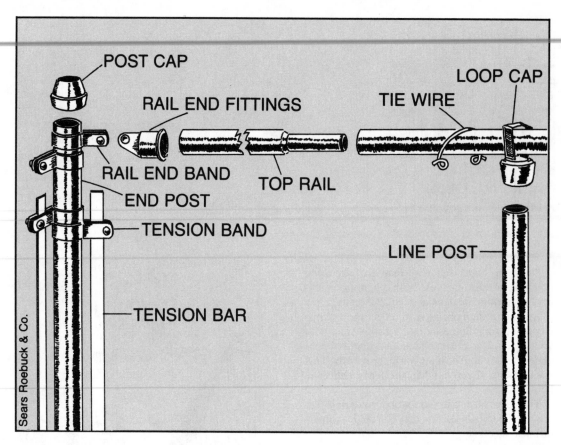

POST CAP

RAIL END FITTINGS

TIE WIRE

LOOP CAP

RAIL END BAND

TOP RAIL

END POST

TENSION BAND

LINE POST

TENSION BAR

Sears Roebuck & Co.

Parts for a chain link fence are easily assembled.

Chain Link Fence

For a strong, practically indestructible fence that requires little maintenance, the chain link fence is your best bet. Compared with other fencing, however, the chain link fence is expensive. Of course, high initial cost is somewhat balanced by the longer life of chain link over wood.

Steel or aluminum chain link fencing are especially good for enclosing yards, play areas, swimming pools and pet areas. Best of all, you can construct the chain link fence with a few basic tools.

The materials you need to construct a chain link fence depend upon many variables: type, purpose, size, length, location, budget and manufacturer. Most chain link fences use the chain-line fabric, a top rail, link posts, loop caps, terminal posts, tension bar, brace band, rail ends, post caps, gates and hinges, and carriage bolts to fasten all the pieces together.

First, survey your property lines to ensure that you locate your chain link fence properly. Professionals recommend that the fence be placed 4 in. inside the property line.

Next, determine the location of terminal (end, corner and gate) posts. Distance between gate posts is determined by adding the actual width of the gate, adding an allowance for hinges and latches (3¾ in. for single walk gates and 5½ in. for double drive gates).

Mark all posts with crayon or chalk for the correct height of fence you are installing. Set terminal posts 2 in. higher and line posts 2 in. lower than the width of the chain-link fabric. Set the terminal posts in concrete using a carpenter's level to make sure they are plumb. Crown all post footings for good water drainage.

Mark the grade line on all posts measuring from the top down. Then measure the distance between terminal posts and check the line post spacing chart for the exact distance to allow between line posts.

Now stretch a mason's line between the outsides of terminal posts. The line posts should be lined up so that when they are set in the center of their holes, their centers will line up with the terminal post centers. When this is done, dig the line post holes and set the line posts.

Move your mason's line up the terminal posts to a point 4 in. below the post tops so that you can align the height of line posts. You can adjust the post height before the concrete sets by simply pulling it up or tapping it down. Make sure the line posts do not move from plumb when you adjust the line.

The next step in installing a chain link fence is to apply fittings to terminal posts. This includes (bottom to top) a tension bar and bands, top rail and rail ends, brace band and post cap.

After assembling the framework, unroll the chain-link fabric on the ground along the fence line starting at a terminal post. Then slide the tension bar through the last link in the fabric and attach this combination to the terminal post using the tension band and bolts provided. The fabric should be on the outside face of all posts.

Stretch the fabric from the terminal post already attached to the opposite terminal post. Insert the tension bar in the end of the fabric and attach the fence stretcher to the bar. As you stretch the fabric, test it for tension; it should give slightly. Locate the top of the fabric about ½ in. above the top rail to insure proper height. Once the fabric is sufficiently tight, remove excess fabric and connect the tension bar to the post with tension bands. Then fasten the fabric to the top rail and line posts with tie wires spaced about 18 in. apart.

Once the fence is completed, install male hinges on one of the gate posts, hanging the top hinge upside down to prevent the gate from being lifted off. Loosely apply female hinges to the gate frame and slip them onto the male hinges. Set hinges to allow for full swing of the gate, then align the top of the gate with the top of the fence. Tighten all hinges securely. Finally, install the gate latch.

Shadow Box Fence

If you'd like to dress up your board fence with a decorative and functional addition, consider the shadow box. It can be installed in existing fences but is better designed into a new fence, preferably not a boundary fence.

The 2×6 pieces form the frame through which you can see the plants. They also help support the cap. Vertical 2×4s support the shadow box and connect to the fence with horizontal 2×4 rails into which fence boards and caps are nailed.

First, install the 2×6 vertical frame members. Next, position and nail vertical 2×4 box posts, prenailing two corner 2×4s at 90° angles, and attach them with horizontal rails on the top and bottom. The edges of the shadow box should rest on the ground.

Once the vertical and horizontal 2×4s are in place, attach fence boards as shown. Then add the 2×6 caps.

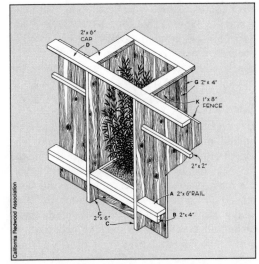

An alcove for a planter *(above)* in your fence breaks up a monotonous design. Outdoor light *(below)* can be installed on a fence for functional variety.

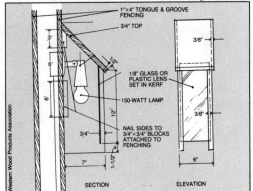

Materials List
Shadow Box Fence

Key	Pcs	Size and description (use)
A	1	2×6×96″ rail
B	1	2×4×96″ rail support
C	2	2×6×72″ frames
D	1	2×6×?″ cap to fit
E	2	2×6×?″ side caps to fit
F	1	2×6×?″ rear cap to fit
G	2	2×4×72″ posts
H	4	2×4×?″ side rails to fit
J	2	2×4×?″ rear rails to fit
K	12	1×8×72″ fence boards

Fasteners:
Galvanized 12d and 16d nails

Tools:
Saw, hammer, level and measuring tape

Deck Design and Construction

Though deck construction is work, it isn't very difficult—as long as you do the project step-by-step in easy-to-manage stages. You'll find the material in this chapter a valuable addition to the basic deck construction tips and other deck projects you'll find in Volume 7 of your set of the *Popular Mechanics Do-it-Yourself Encyclopedia* books.

Deck Footings

Deck footings support the deck posts. They can rest on the ground, but for most decks they are buried in the ground. Footings may be either concrete blocks, pre-cast pier blocks or poured concrete. A footing should be at least twice the size of the post it supports.

Deck Posts

Deck posts are the vertical members which rest on the footings and support the beams. The length of the posts is critical to establishing the height of the deck. Timbers, 4×4-in. and larger, are most popular for deck posts. If your deck must hold large crowds, deep snow or other heavy loads, or if the deck is elevated, larger posts and cross bracing may be necessary to prevent lateral movement.

Deck Beams

Deck beams rest on the posts and support the joists. For some low decks, beams may rest directly on the footings. Beams 4×6-in. and greater are common.

The end beam that is attached to the house is called a *ledger*. The ledger should be nailed or bolted into the house framing or into the concrete foundation. Fasteners should penetrate at least 1½ in. into the framing or foundation.

Deck Joists

Joists rest on the beams and support the decking. Install them on edge, with one of the thin sides resting on the beams. At the side of the house, support the joists with a ledger.

Decking

The decking is the wood surface on which you will walk. Install it horizontally on top of the deck joists. Most decking is 2×4 or 2×6 pressure-treated or decay-resistant wood. Decking should span no more than 24 inches. If you plan to install a large permanent planter, hot tub, spa or other heavy object, make sure you build in extra support.

Details of deck construction showing how posts, ledger, beams and decking are attached.

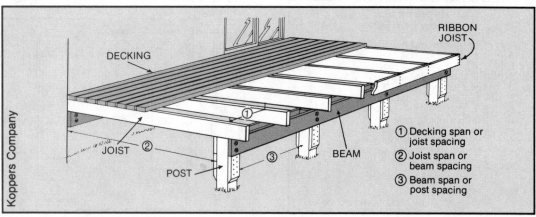

USE A 10 PENNY NAIL FOR SPACER

Nail decking to joists.

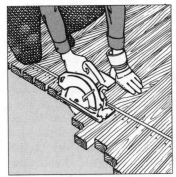

Trim decking to length with power saw.

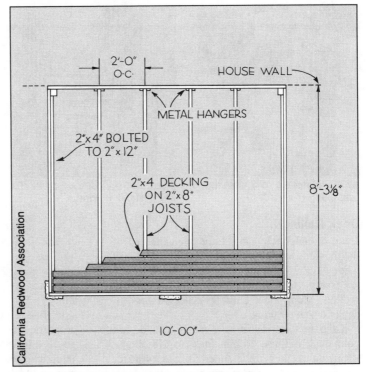

California Redwood Association

2'-0" O.C.

HOUSE WALL

METAL HANGERS

2"x 4" BOLTED TO 2"x 12"

2"x4 DECKING ON 2"x 8" JOISTS

8'-3⅛"

10'-00"

Joists provide support for decking. Determine joist spacing by the load on the decking.

Decking is installed on the joists. Extra 2×4s bolted to end joists provide a nailing surface for decking.

Metal hangers on ledger support the joists.

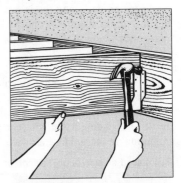

Bolt posts to joists and beam.

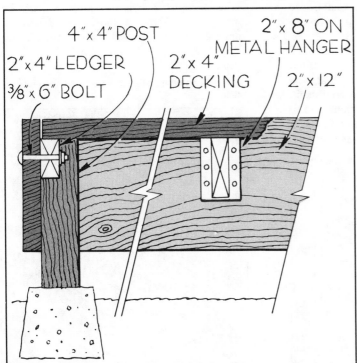

4"x 4" POST

2"x 4" LEDGER

⅜"x 6" BOLT

2"x 4" DECKING

2"x 8" ON METAL HANGER

2"x 12"

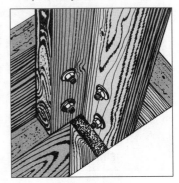

Stairs can make a deck more accessible to your yard.

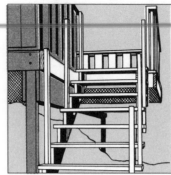

Install stair stringer then treads and posts for railings.

Nail treads to stringers using spacer between boards.

Deck Railings

Even though deck railings are often the last of the finishing touches, you need to consider them when you're planning your deck. Railings are necessary for any deck over 18 in. off the ground. Many local building codes require all decks to have railings.

Keep human nature in mind as you design your deck railings. Design them to discourage sitting unless they are intended for that purpose, and make sure they are sturdy barriers that don't obstruct the view.

Securely fasten railings to your deck. Bolt rail posts to joists or beams, or design them as an extension of the deck post. Toenailing the rail posts to the deck surface is not adequate. Use vertical grain wood for the rail cap for better resistance to splitting and weathering.

Deck Benches

Deck benches are other elements that you should design into and not add onto your deck. Keep in mind that the best bench height is 15 to 18 in., depending upon whether you will install cushions on them. Here are two simple designs:

The built-in bench is actually part of the deck railing. The length of the back and seat boards varies according to your plan. Repeat the seat supports every two feet to make the bench sturdy. The seat slats are 1×2 boards on edge and spaced ½ in. apart. Bench supports extend from the railings' posts which are, in turn, bolted to deck joists and beams. The horizontal bench supports are pairs of 2×4×48-in. lumber between which posts and legs are installed. Each leg is attached to the decking using a metal angle bracket. Make sure the railing is strong enough to support the bench and the weight of people leaning against the back of the bench.

The second bench is moveable and can be constructed easily in a short time. It's made from a 2×12×96-in. board braced with a 2×4.

Rail placed on side of post discourages sitting on it.

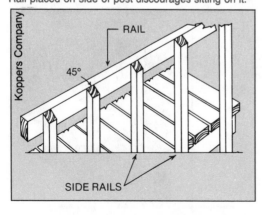

Koppers Company

RAIL

45°

SIDE RAILS

Deck rail can be modified to include a bench for sitting.

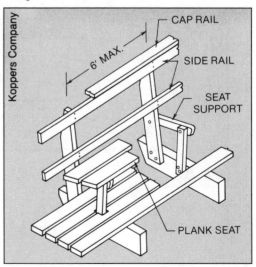

Koppers Company

CAP RAIL

6' MAX.

SIDE RAIL

SEAT SUPPORT

PLANK SEAT

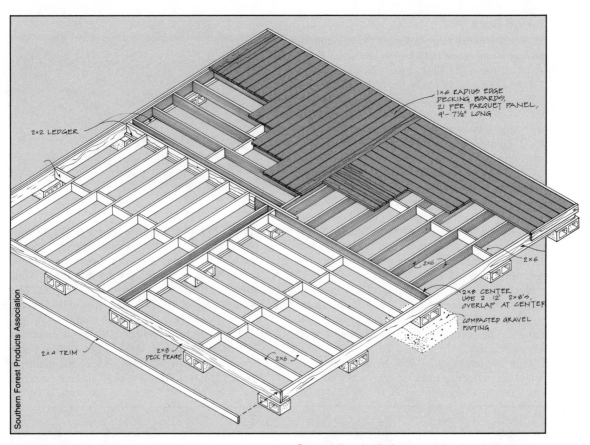

Labels on illustration:

2×2 LEDGER

1×6 RADIUS EDGE DECKING BOARDS, 21 PER PARQUET PANEL, 9'-7½" LONG

2×6

2×6

2×8 CENTER USE 2 12' 2×8'S, OVERLAP AT CENTER

COMPACTED GRAVEL FOOTING

2×4 TRIM

2×8 DECK FRAME

2×6

Southern Forest Products Association

Construction details for ground level deck that uses blocks rather than posts.

Ground-Level Deck

Here are some specific plans for decks that you can modify to fit your own needs.

To construct a ground-level deck, first determine its exact location. Omit 2×4 trim pieces on the sides that will adjoin your house or other structure. Install concrete footings or compacted gravel footings as illustrated. Remember that the top of the footings and bottoms of concrete blocks should be at ground level.

Build the perimeter deck frame by cutting two 2×8s to 19 ft., 6 in. (234 in.) and two more to 19 ft., 3 in. (231 in.). Make a square frame using 12d nails and construction adhesive.

Next, install the center support using two 2×12×144-in. boards overlapped at the center. Position them along the center line of the deck frame; nail the overlap and attach the center support to the deck frame using 10d nails. Complete the basic support frame by cutting two 2×8s to fit between the deck frame and the center support. Toenail these to the overlapping 2×8 sections of the center support.

Select the deck board direction for your parquet pattern in each of the four quadrants.

Attach 2×2 ledgers to the 2×8 deck frame and center supports. Ledgers support both ends of the 2×6 joists. Be sure combined ledger and 2×6 joist height is flush with the top of the 2×8s. Now attach the ledger to the 2×8s using construction adhesive and galvanized lag screws. Drill 3/16-in. holes to receive five screws per ledger, spacing them about 18 in. apart.

Install 2×6 joists 16 in. o.c. perpendicular to the selected direction of the deck boards using 10d nails. Make sure all members are square as you install. Install 2×6 bridging between the joists along the centerline of each quadrant. Stagger their placement to make nailing easier. Tops of bridging and joists should be flush.

Next, begin arranging 1×6×120-in. deck boards, bark side up, starting at the center of the deck and building the parquet pattern to each edge. Allow the board length to hang over the 2×8 perimeter deck frame.

Once you have attached all 21 deck boards, cut all the ends flush with the 2×8 perimeter frame. Then attach the 2×4 trim pieces to the 2×8 frame using 10d nails.

Raised Deck

For many homes, a raised deck is the solution to moving living space outdoors at low cost. Here are plans for a 10×12-ft. raised deck and stairs that you can modify easily for your needs.

Wood can either be decay-resistant redwood or CCA pressure-treated wood. Use .40 pounds per cubic foot preservative retention level for wood contacting the earth and .25 lb./cu. ft. otherwise.

First, determine the exact location and height of the deck and steps. Locate the 4×4 post positions and dig holes for setting them in concrete. Use stakes, line and level to aid positioning of the posts. Use 4×4×96-in. posts at the end of stairs and where posts don't extend above the deck surface. Allow sufficient time for the concrete to set before continuing.

Next, determine the location of the finished deck surface, (the top of the 1×6-in. deck boards) and mark all deck and stair posts. Use the line and level to help you determine this reference mark.

Trim the intermediate 4×4-in. posts to 1 in. below the reference mark on the corner posts.

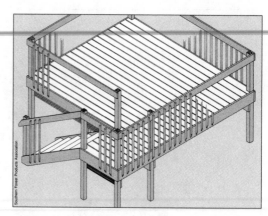

Attach 2×8×144-in. deck beams to the 4×4-in. posts. Through-bolt the beams to the posts using three ½×6-in. bolts per post. Countersink these using the ⅞-in. bit ⅜ in. deep into the 4×4-in. posts, then drill through with the ½-in. bit. The bottom edge of the 2×8 beam should be 15½ in. below the reference mark you made earlier.

Cut two beams from the 2×8×96-in. beams to 44½ in. each. Attach them to the 4×4-in. posts beneath the stair platform. Where the platform adjoins the deck, through-bolt this beam and the

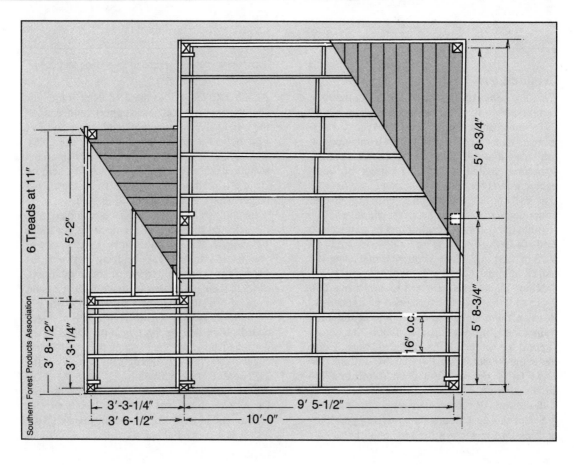

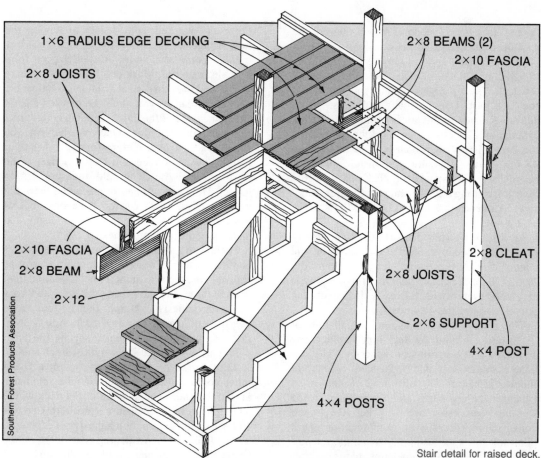

1×6 RADIUS EDGE DECKING

2×8 JOISTS

2×8 BEAMS (2)

2×10 FASCIA

2×10 FASCIA

2×8 BEAM

2×12

2×8 CLEAT

2×8 JOISTS

2×6 SUPPORT

4×4 POST

4×4 POSTS

Southern Forest Products Association

Stair detail for raised deck.

deck beam to 4×4-in. posts using 8-in. bolts. Attach the other stair platform beam to 4×4-in. posts using three ½×6-in. countersunk bolts at two locations. Check for level and square.

The next step is to install the 2×8-in. floor joists. From the 2×8×120-in. material, cut two end joists 110 in. long to fit between the 4×4-in. posts. Toenail the posts using 12d nails making sure the outside face of the joist is flush with the outside edge of the 4×4-in. posts. Cut six of the 2×8×120-in. lumber to 117 inches. Arrange them 16-in. o.c. from the end of the deck opposite the stair platform. Toenail them to the 2×8-in. beams using 12d nails.

Now cut and install members that span the deck and stair platform. Cut the two 2×8×168-in. boards 156¼ in. long. Toenail them to 2×8 beams 16-in. o.c. using 12d nails. Cut two end joists for the stair platform 35¾ in. long from the 2×8×144-in. stock. Toenail one to the 4×4-in. posts at the top of the stairs and the other flush with the outside of the deck. Then cut one piece 43 in. long and attach it to the 4×4-in. posts just opposite the one at the head of the stairs using 12d nails.

Materials List Raised Deck		
Pcs	**Size and description**	
7	4×4×120″ lumber	
3	4×4×96″ lumber	
3	2×12×96″ lumber	
2	2×10×144″ lumber	
3	2×10×120″ lumber	
4	2×8×144″ lumber	
9	2×8×144″ lumber	
3	2×6×144″ lumber	
1	2×6×168″ lumber	
1	2×6×120″ lumber	
62	2×2×96″ lumber	
22	1×6×144″ lumber	
7	1×6×120″ lumber	

Fasteners:
8d, 10d, 12d galvanized nails
¼×4″ galvanized lag screws
½×6″ galvanized bolts with nuts and washers
½×8″ galvanized bolts with nuts and washers

Tools:
Circular or crosscut saw, hammer, drill with ⅞″, ½″ and ³⁄₁₆″ bits, socket wrench, stakes, line, level, square, carpenter's tape, ladder and miter box

Cut bridging to brace the joists along the deck's centerline from the last 2×8×144-in. board. End nail the joists to the bridging using 10d nails. Use scrap 2×8 material to make cleats for the deck board support. Attach them to the 4×4-in. posts using 10d nails.

The next major step is to install decking. Start by attaching a 2×10×120-in. fascia to one end of the deck. The top edge should extend 1 in. above the 2×8 joist. Use 12d nails and construction adhesive to attach the fascia to the posts. Then arrange all 22 1×6×144-in. deck boards across the 2×8 joists. Notch boards to fit around the 4×4-in. posts. Be sure you install the deck boards bark side up. Attach deck boards to the floor joists using 8d nails and construction adhesive. Trim ends that extend beyond the 4×4-in. post's outer edge.

To install the stair platform decking, simply repeat the procedure. Start at the end facing the stairs. Cut three equal lengths from the 1×6×120-in. deck material. Once the platform is in place, evenly trim the ends flush with the outside edge of the 4×4 posts.

The trim is next. Complete installation of 2×10 fascia around the deck's perimeter using 10d nails and construction adhesive. The top edge of the 2×10 should be flush with the top of the deck boards. Install the 2×6 top rails. Chamfer the top edges and attach them to the 4×4-in. posts using two 4-in. lag screws and construction adhesive at each location. Drill pilot holes using a 3/16-in. bit. From the remaining 2×6×144-in. board, cut a top rail for the stair banister. Chamfer and attach to the posts with 4-in. lag screws and construction adhesive.

From this material, cut a ledger to support the stair stringers.

Next come the stairs. Cut stringers from 2×12-in. material. Mark one leg of your square at 6 in. and the other leg at 11 inches. Outline the riser and tread as you slide the marked square along one edge of the 2×12, keeping both marks aligned with the edge. Once you've cut one stringer, use it as a pattern for the other two. Notch all three to receive a 2×6-in. ledger at the platform. The notch should measure 1½×4 inches. Hold one stringer in place and mark the location of the ledger's top edge on the 4×4 post. Attach the ledger to the post using 12d nails and construction adhesive.

Toenail the stringers to the ledger and stair platform using 12d nails. Cut stair treads as shown using the remaining 1×6×120-in. boards. Attach these stringers using 8d nails and construction adhesive. Notch the bottom tread board to fit around the 4×4 post. Add a 2×10 fascia to the outside of the stairs using 10d nails.

Prepare 2×2-in. railing spindles. Each spindle is 42 in. long with a 45° cut on the ends. Use a miter box to cut the ends. Attach the spindles 5 in. o.c. on stairs and all sides of the deck where a complete railing enclosure is desired. Use two 10d nails and construction adhesive at each end. Tack a line 2 in. below the top edge of the railing to aid the even placement of spindle tops.

Finally, apply a coat of water repellent sealer to all exposed surfaces.

Construction plans for a 12′×16′ hot tub deck.

Check Building Codes

Deck plans shown in this chapter may not meet all requirements of local building codes for construction. Check with your local authorities or a structural architect before you start a project.

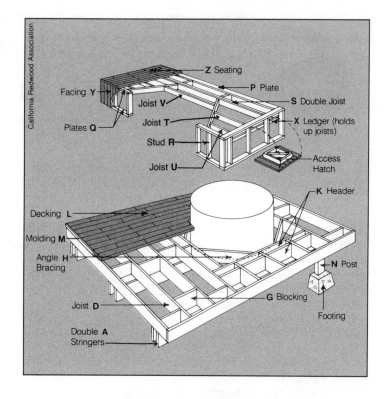

Framing details for a 12'×16' hot tub deck, showing the raised seating area. Plans show framing for a 6'-diameter hot tub. Modify the framing if your hot tub is larger or smaller.

Hot Tub Deck

Here are plans for constructing a 12×16 ft. hot tub deck with raised seating area. You can use pressure-treated wood, but most do-it-yourselfers select decay-resistant redwood or cedar.

Construct the hot tub deck using procedures described earlier in this chapter. Construction stages are: footings, posts, stringers, joists, headers, decking then molding. The raised seating area houses the plumbing and stores accessories. The access hatch consists of 2×4s attached to a simple box frame.

Trim your hot tub deck to fit the tub by tracing the deck with a scribe made of a block with a pencil secured to it. Cut the curve of the tub on the block with a jig or keyhole saw. Then rough cut the decking so it almost touches the side of the tub. Trace with the scribe, then cut, nail and trim.

You'll find other hot tub and swimming pool decks in Chapter 9 of this book. You'll get many other ideas for these decks from the illustrations shown in that chapter.

A deck can provide for outdoor entertaining and relaxation whether you're planning on a deck for your hot tub, spa or swimming pool or you're planning to add one to enhance your yard and extend your living space outdoors.

Materials List
Hot Tub Deck
DECK

Key	Pcs	Size and description (use)
A	4	2×10×192″ stringers
B	2	2×10×84″ stringers
C	2	2×10×24″ stringers
D	6	2×6×144″ joists
E	1	2×6×72″ joists
F	6	2×6×26″ joists
G	12	2×6×24″ blocking
H	4	2×6×36″ angle bracing
J	2	2×6×96″ headers
K	2	2×6×192″ headers
L		2×4″×370′ decking
M		1×2″×56′ molding
N	9	4×4×height posts

RAISED SEATING AREA

Key	Pcs	Size and description (use)
P	2	2×4×144″ plates
Q	6	2×4×72″ plates
R	26	2×4×24″ studs
S	2	2×6×144″ joists
T	2	2×6×48″ joists
U	2	2×6×36″ joists
V	1	2×6×44″ joist
W	2	2×6×18″ joists
X	2	2×6×72″ ledgers
Y		1×6″×124′ facing
Z		2×6″×124′ decking

Fasteners:
16d galvanized nails
3/8×4″ galvanized lag screws and washers

6 Sheds and Storage Buildings

A building that provides adequate, handy work areas and storage space requires careful thought. Begin planning your storage building by developing a list of work areas and storage needs. Sheds and storage buildings could house a garden tractor, gardening tools, power mower and supplies, rakes, brooms, shovels, hoes, axes, lawn trimmers and edgers, wheelbarrows, extension ladders, stepladders, hoses, sprinklers, paint brushes, window washing equipment, storm windows and screens, bicycles, wagons, sleds, skis, a canoe, a snowmobile, woodworking shop and equipment, a freezer, root vegetables, canned food, garbage cans, recycled materials, junk and much more. Other projects for building backyard structures like those shown in this chapter are explained in Volume 27 of your *Popular Mechanics Do-it-Yourself Encyclopedia*.

Basic 8′×10′ shed is an easy construction project. This shed provides plenty of storage space for garden tools as well as normal household accumulations.

Planning Your Storage Building

Keep in mind as you plan your storage building that, over the years, your needs will change. This year's hobbies and activities may be next year's memories. Also remember that no matter how much storage space you have, it's not enough. You will soon have it filled. So provide for an open flexible storage building that you can modify to include a recreation vehicle, workshop, shelving or other space-takers.

The first consideration to determine storage space needs is convenience. You can find a few moments for garden work at nearly any time if the tools and materials are nearby, but if the work takes another hour of gathering and putting away materials, you'll probably postpone the job. Plan for maintenance as well as for convenience. Install a small workbench for parts and tools in any storage building that you'll use for equipment. This is especially true for seasonal equipment such as snowmobiles and lawn equipment that should be checked over before you use them each season. You can reduce space needs by installing ceiling racks for seasonal equipment and by planning for equipment swaps: the lawnmower comes out and the snow blower gets put in its place.

Safety is an important design consideration for storage buildings, especially if you have children. Keep storage buildings securely locked. If you're storing poisons, herbicides, paints, inflammable liquids or other dangerous materials, keep them locked up separately within your storage building.

Remember to plan for adequate lighting so you won't stumble over materials as you enter from the bright sunlight. Lighting can come from windows, skylights or electrical lights. Artificial lighting, however, requires that you run electrical service to your storage building at additional effort and cost—usually only for minimal use.

Metal Storage Sheds

Small storage buildings, sometimes called sheds, are economical and easy to put up. They offer low-cost storage but usually don't provide as much security as other structures.

Storage sheds are generally made of metal or wood and vary in size from 6×8 to 12×18 feet. They can be built without a floor, with a simple wood floor or placed on a concrete slab. Their most practical use is for storing equipment.

If you've selected a metal storage shed, check the strength and durability of doors. Also make sure you anchor the shed securely. An unanchored storage shed with thin doors is an open invitation to burglars. Keep in mind, too, that most metal storage sheds have low roof lines and are not strong enough for hanging tools and materials.

The metal storage shed normally has six phases of construction: pre-assembly, floor frames, wall assembly, roof support, door installation, and roof assembly. Carefully follow the plans that come with your shed. Common tool requirements are a tape measure, spade or shovel, straight-edge board, carpenter's level, saw, hammer, wrench, electric drill and any lumber needed to construct foundation forms.

Wooden Storage Shed

Here are plans for an 8×10 ft. storage shed made from wood. You can modify the plans for a 9×12, 12×16 or other size shed.

If you won't be storing heavy equipment or materials, you can reduce construction costs by substituting a ¾-in. exterior grade plywood or 1×6s for the 2×6s in the board floor. If so, you'll need three 4×8 plywood sheets or 18 boards each 1×6×120-in. to replace the 2×6×120-in. boards.

As with any outdoor structure, the first step is to determine the location of the structure. Then install your foundation or pier footings.

The base is next, either attached to a concrete foundation or to wooden skids. Trim the two 2×8×120-in. boards to 119 in. and four of the 2×8×96-in. boards to 92 in. long. Build the 2×8 base frame with these boards using 10d nails and construction adhesive. Use a double 2×8 on each side. Attach the base frame to the foundation using 12d nails and construction adhesive, making sure the base is level and square.

Install seven 2×8×92-in. floor joists 16-in. o.c. on the base frame using 10d nails for end nailing and 12d nails for toenailing. Check each floor joist and frame joint for square.

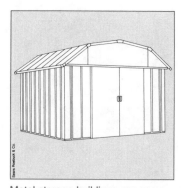

Metal storage buildings are easy to assemble and low in cost.

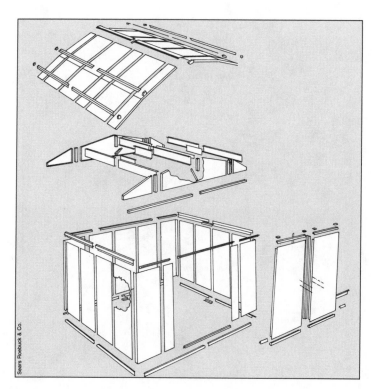

Easy-to-follow instructions come with most metal storage sheds making assembly simply a matter of fitting numbered pieces together.

Next attach a 2×4×119-in. plate to the top front and rear edge of the base frame using 10d nails. Install 18 floor boards each 2×6×119-in. to the base frame and floor joists using 10d nails and construction adhesive.

Fabricate the rear stud wall using 2×4×91½-in. lumber. Use a double 2×4 on each end, with studs 16-in. o.c., plus an extra stud at the center. Nail the studs to 2×4×119-in. top and bottom members using 10d nails. Attach the finished wall frame to the 2×4 plate using 10d nails and construction adhesive.

The two side walls are next. Fabricate them using 2×4×91½-in. lumber 16-in. o.c. Start at the center of the 88-in. wall section and space studs as shown on the drawing. Nail the studs to 2×4 top and bottom members using 10d nails. Then attach the finished wall frame to ends of the floor boards using 10d nails and construction adhesive.

For the front wall, also use 2×4×91½-in. lumber. End sections are double-end 2×4s with a center stud nailed to common 2×4s top and bottom. The finished wall frame is 34¾-in. wide. Attach the wall to the 2×4 plate using 10d nails and construction adhesive. At the doors, the inside 2×4s are cut 81 in. from top of base frame to support the double 2×6×51-in. header over the door opening. Use 10d nails.

Connect the side wall frame sections with 2×4×95-in. top plates. Join the front and rear wall frame sections with 2×4×112-in. top plates using 10d nails. These top plates become the rafter supports. Check the wall framing for square before continuing.

Materials List
Heavy Duty Wooden Storage Shed

Pcs	Size and description
2	2×8×120" lumber
11	2×8×96" lumber
7	2×6×144" lumber
18	2×6×120" lumber
6	2×4×120" lumber
49	2×4×96" lumber
4	1×8×120" lumber
1	1×6×120" lumber
2	1×4×96" lumber
8	1×2×96" lumber
11	48×96×½" exterior plywood siding
	120 sq. ft. 15 lb. roofing felt
5	48×96×½" exterior sheathing plywood
2	10' galvanized eave drip
4	6' galvanized standard eave drip
	120 sq. ft. fiberglass or asphalt shingle

Fasteners:
6d, 8d, 10d, 12d galvanized nails
3 pr. galvanized butt hinges
Construction adhesive
Door handles and closure hardware
Roofing nails

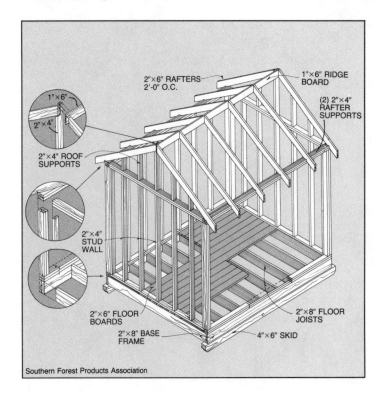

2"×6" RAFTERS 2'-0" O.C.
1"×6" RIDGE BOARD
1"×6"
2"×4"
(2) 2"×4" RAFTER SUPPORTS
2"×4" ROOF SUPPORTS
2"×4" STUD WALL
2"×6" FLOOR BOARDS
2"×8" BASE FRAME
2"×8" FLOOR JOISTS
4"×6" SKID

Southern Forest Products Association

A 1×2 batten (below lock hasp) serves as a stop at the edge of door.

Basic 8'×10' shed frame, showing construction details for ridge board, top plate and sill. 2×4s are used for walls, 2×6s for rafters. Plywood sheets can be substituted for individual boards in the flooring.

Pour concrete for footings into cardboard tubes, placing anchor bolts before concrete sets.

Install frame on top of footings with anchor bolts.

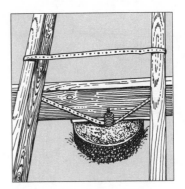

Install joists between outside framing, anchored to footings with metal straps to anchor bolts.

Cut rafters from the 2×6×144-in. stock. Then cut two 2×4×33-in. ridge board supports and notch them to receive 2×6 end rafters. Toenail them into the center of the side walls using 12d nails. Attach the 1×6 ridge board using 8d nails, making sure it extends 1 in. above the 2×4 center support.

Install the roof rafters, as shown, 24-in. o.c. Nail them to the ridge board using 10d nails and toenail the other ends to the rafter support using 12d nails. You have completely framed your wooden storage shed.

Taller footings can compensate for uneven terrain. An additional support under the floor joists may be necessary to keep joists level.

Decorative wind vane installed on top of the shed can be built or purchased ready-made.

Cutaway plan showing finishing touches for the 8′×10′ shed. On level terrain, skids placed under the joists on each end can be used instead of footings to let you move the shed with a tractor to different locations in your yard.

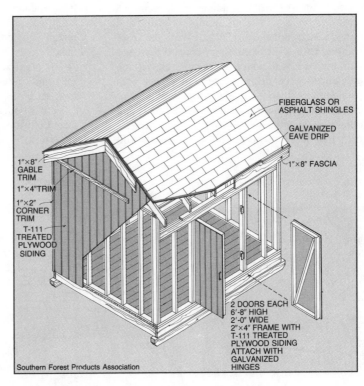

FIBERGLASS OR ASPHALT SHINGLES

GALVANIZED EAVE DRIP

1″×8″ FASCIA

1″×8″ GABLE TRIM

1″×4″TRIM

1″×2″ CORNER TRIM

T-111 TREATED PLYWOOD SIDING

2 DOORS EACH 6′-8″ HIGH 2′-0″ WIDE 2″×4″ FRAME WITH T-111 TREATED PLYWOOD SIDING ATTACH WITH GALVANIZED HINGES

Southern Forest Products Association

Corner blocks ensure frame remains rigid.

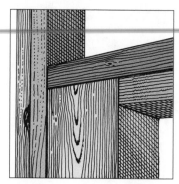

Install headers over doors and windows.

Rafter detail shown birds-mouth cut on rafter.

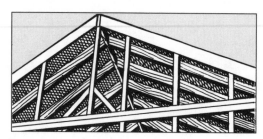

Complete rafter framing.

To finish, enclose the wall framing with exterior plywood siding panels. Attach to studs using 6d nails and construction adhesive. Attach 1×8 fascia to ends of rafters using 6d nails and construction adhesive. Then cover the roof framing with ½-in. sheathing plywood fastened with 6d nails. Add a layer of roofing felt. Attach galvanized eave drips to the roof edges with roofing nails. Install shingles with roofing nails.

To complete the trim work (using 8d nails and construction adhesive), install 1×2-in. corner trim to cover the plywood siding joints. Add 1×4×96-in. trim to cover siding panel joints on side walls between corner trim. Cut 1×8-in. material for exterior gable trim, matching the profile of the rafters, flush with the roofing edges and 1×8 fascia.

Build the two doors by cutting two panels of plywood siding 24×80-in. Attach the 2×4 frame as shown, making sure that the hinge side of the frame is flush with the edge of the panel. Recess the top and door handle side of the frame 1 in. from the edge of the panel. Recess the bottom member of the door frame 2 in. to clear floor boards when the door is closed. Add a diagonal 2×4 brace. Attach siding to the frame using 6d nails and construction adhesive. Hang the doors using galvanized butt hinges and screws. Then install your choice of door handles and locking hasp.

The plans also provide for an optional 36×48-in. ramp to help you move heavy equipment in and out more easily.

Your wooden storage shed is complete. Apply a coat of water repellent sealer to the floor and to all exterior wood surfaces.

Install windows and doors then put up the siding.

Cover roof using felt and asphalt shingles.

Completed roofing with trim installed.

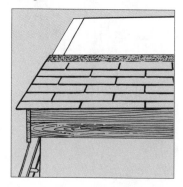

Garden Storage Shed

Maybe you don't need a large shed. You might prefer a shed to store just garden or pool maintenance tools and possibly some children's toys. Here's a simple construction project that you can build from six 4×8 sheets of exterior-grade plywood. The dimensions shown on the panel layouts will build a 32-sq. ft. garden storage shed.

The ¾-in. plywood does not need as much bracing and support as other building materials. In addition to the 6 sheets of plywood, you'll also need some 2×4 pressure-treated lumber for the shed's base and some 2×2s and 2×3s to frame-in each plywood section. If you plan to roof the shed, you'll need about 8 ft. of roofing paper 56 in. wide.

Begin construction by carefully cutting the left and right sides from two plywood panels as shown in the panel layouts below. Frame each of the two sides by nailing a 2×4 to the bottom edge, using 6d galvanized nails. Then put a length of 2×2 along each side, mark and cut the top angles, and fasten them to the plywood. Mark and cut another 2×2 to go along the top edge.

The back of the shed is built in four sections. At the top of each of the 3-ft., 4-in. plywood panel sections install a 2×3, 4 ft. long that will also serve as the bottom support for the smaller 1-ft., 2-in. back panel top piece as shown in the shed drawing.

When framing the back of the door panels, don't forget to install the 2×2 across the bottom at least 3½-in. up from the lower edge so it will clear the base 2×4 when closed.

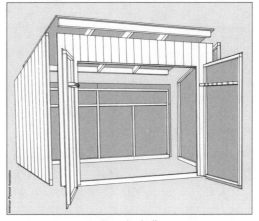

Garden storage shed can be built from 4'×8' plywood sheets.

After you have cut and framed all plywood panels you can assemble the shed. Drill clearance holes for 5/16-in. carriage bolts through the 2×2 end pieces where they will butt against each other. Two carriage bolts to hold a 4-ft. section will probably be enough. Caulk all joints, then finish with paint or stain.

Shelving and tool racks can easily be installed inside to organize your storage space.

Panel layouts for constructing the plywood shed. Careful planning and cutting can keep waste to a minimum.

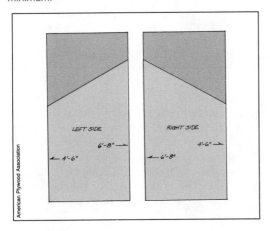

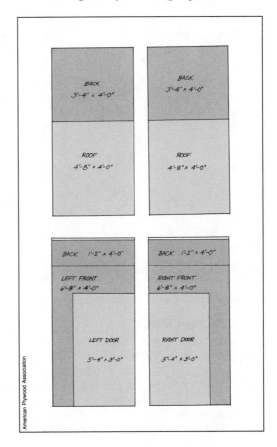

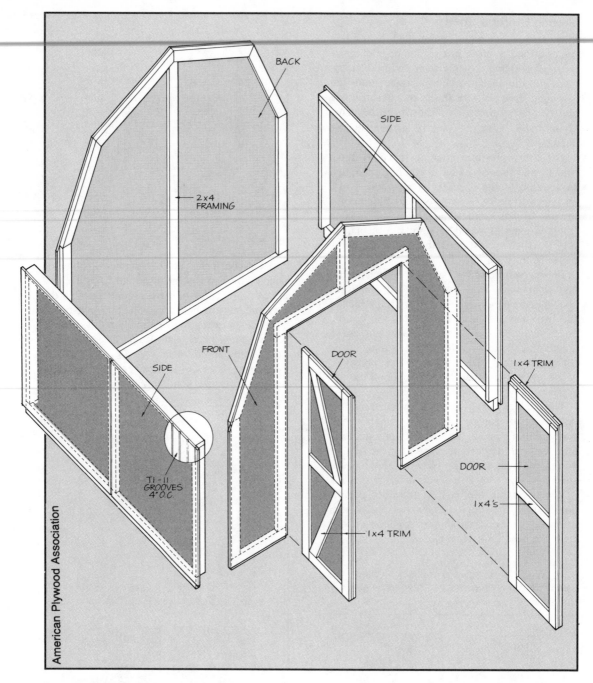

BACK

SIDE

2x4
FRAMING

FRONT

SIDE

TI-II
GROOVES
4" O.C.

DOOR

1x4 TRIM

DOOR

1x4's

1x4 TRIM

American Plywood Association

Construction details for small storage barn.

Small Storage Barn

A more decorative shed is the small storage barn with gambrel roof. It can be painted to match your house or other outdoor structures or to blend in with surrounding trees. Like the plywood garden shed, construction is simply a matter of framing the inside of plywood panels with 2×4s. Use a 2×6 for the ridge beam.

Depending on the size of storage barn you want, the front and back will require two plywood sections, while each side section can be 4 ft. high and built from a single plywood sheet. Draw a cutting template to scale on a sheet of paper to lay out each section for minimum waste on the plywood sheet. (See panel layouts for the plywood shed.)

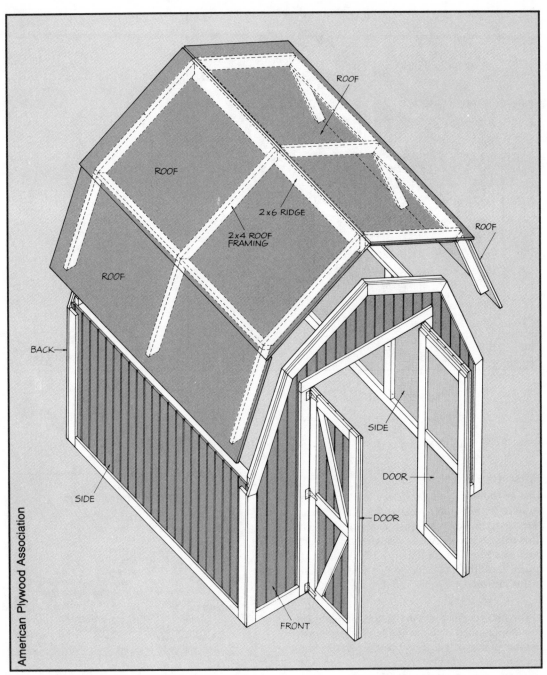

Finishing touches for small storage barn.

When drawing the angles for the gambrel roof on the front and back panels, don't forget that the left and right sections are mirror images of each other. If you're planning to use decorative exterior plywood such as simulated siding, you want both finished surfaces on the exterior of your structure.

When installing the 2×4s to the interior side of the panels, you can use the cut plywood sheets to measure the exact length and angle of each support board. The construction detail drawing shows how these boards should be installed. Use 1×4 lumber to trim the outside edges as shown in the drawing.

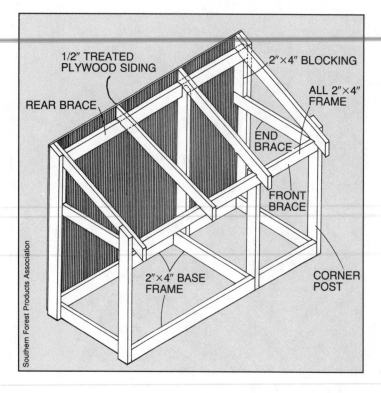

1/2" TREATED PLYWOOD SIDING

REAR BRACE

2"×4" BLOCKING

ALL 2"×4" FRAME

END BRACE

FRONT BRACE

2"×4" BASE FRAME

CORNER POST

Southern Forest Products Association

Framing details for a trash can storage structure.

Trash Can Storage

One of the first outdoor storage buildings constructed by many do-it-yourselfers is also one of the most practical: the trash can storage shed. This plan allows for two compartments. One can hold two 32-gallon trash cans while a second is useful for either recycled papers and materials or for firewood.

The first step in constructing this simple trash can storage shed is to cut the lumber as shown on the material list. Cut three 2×4×26½-in. bottom frame supports from one 8 footer. Cut two 2×4×46½-in., two 2×4×21-in.; and cut one 2×4×26½-in. frame members from one of the 12 footers. From another 12 footer, cut two 2×4×49-in. rear posts and one 2×4×39-in. front corner post, making sure you match the roof slope. Another 12 footer will become a 2×4×44-in. front center support, and a 2×4×35-in. rear center support, notched to receive the 2×4 brace as in the plans. From the remainder, cut the last 2×4×39-in. front corner post.

Materials List
Trash Can Storage Shed

Pcs	Size and description
1	2×4×96" lumber
6	2×4×144" lumber
1	2×4×144" lumber
2	2×4×120" lumber
2	2×2×72" lumber
3	48×96×½" pressure treated siding
1	48×96×½" sheathing plywood (roof)

Fasteners:
6d, 10d galvanized nails; roofing nails
3" galvanized butt hinges with screws
Door handles, hasp and lock
Construction adhesive

Miscellaneous:
Roofing felt
Asphalt or fiberglass shingles
6' galvanized roof ridge

Tools:
Circular or crosscut saw, hammer, square, level, screwdriver and carpenter's tape

Cut the front and rear top supports 2×4×69-in. each from a 12 footer. From each of the two 10-ft. 2×4s cut two rafters 40 in. long and one end brace 26½ in. long, notching as shown.

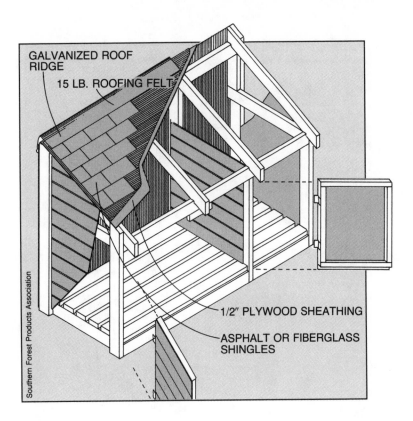

GALVANIZED ROOF RIDGE

15 LB. ROOFING FELT

1/2″ PLYWOOD SHEATHING

ASPHALT OR FIBERGLASS SHINGLES

Southern Forest Products Association

Finishing touches for the trash can storage structure.

To begin construction, first build the 2×4 frame according to the plan. Using 10d nails and construction adhesive, assemble the bottom frame, then add the corner and center posts. Make sure the frame remains level and square.

Attach the end braces to the corner posts using 10d nails. The rear end of the braces should be flush with the rear corner posts. Install the front and rear top supports, fitting them to the notched center posts.

Use scrap 2×4 material to add blocking between end braces and rear top support at the rear corner posts using 10d nails. Toenail rafters into place, evenly spacing them across the span of top supports. You can also attach end rafters to corner posts.

Next, cut a panel of exterior plywood siding 48×72-in. and attach it to the rear corner and center posts with 6d nails. The tops of the plywood panel and posts should be flush.

Cut six floor deck boards from the three remaining 2×4×144-in. boards. Notch the front and rear pieces to fit around the center posts. Then position the floor deck boards 1 in. apart and install using 10d nails and construction adhesive. Make sure you recess the front board ½ in. for the door.

Cut plywood siding panels to fit the sides. Position them between the corner posts and flush with the bottom frame and end rafter. Also from the treated siding, cut a 28-in. square divider panel. Attach it to the center posts using 6d nails.

The next step is to build the doors. Cut two plywood panels 24¾×27-in. each. Attach a 2×2 frame inside the panel using 6d nails and construction adhesive. Make sure the frame is flush with the plywood edges on three sides, allowing siding to extend 2 in. at the bottom to clear the floor deck.

Attach the door posts with galvanized butt hinges. The door siding panel and frame of the unit should be flush when the doors are closed. Install door handles and closure hardware. Then fabricate a door stop using scrap plywood siding and attach it to the front top support with 6d nails.

Finally, install the roof. Attach the ½-in. sheathing plywood to rafters using 6d nails. This panel should cover the area outlined by the corner posts and rafters. Cover with roofing felt, then shingles, using roofing nails. Attach the galvanized roof ridge to the rear corner and center posts using 6d nails.

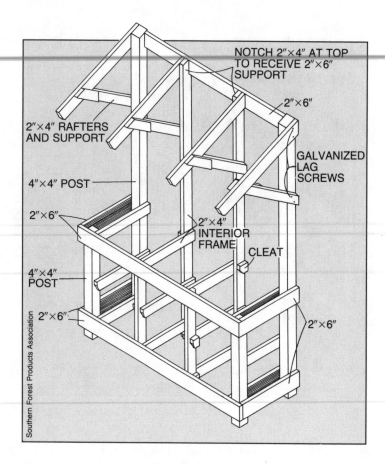

NOTCH 2″×4″ AT TOP
TO RECEIVE 2″×6″
SUPPORT

2″×6″

2″×4″ RAFTERS
AND SUPPORT

GALVANIZED
LAG
SCREWS

4″×4″ POST

2″×6″

2″×4″
INTERIOR
FRAME

CLEAT

4″×4″
POST

2″×6″

2″×6″

Southern Forest Products Association

Framing for a potting shed.

Potting Shed

Gardeners enjoy having an outdoor work station for potting plants and for storing tools and supplies. This potting shed design provides both. It has been designed as a free-standing structure, but you can also attach it to an existing fence, garage or other building. Use pressure-treated lumber: .40 preservative retention level for ground contact lumber and .25 for other applications.

To begin, cut two 34×4×39½-in. posts and two 4×4×104½-in. posts, making an angle cut on one end to match the slope of the roof.

Cut four 2×6×26-in. outside frame pieces. Join the 2×6×72-in. units to the front 4×4 posts, then join the front and rear posts together with the smaller outside pieces. Make sure the basic frame remains square and level.

Attach the 2×4 frame supports to the inside of the 4×4 posts using 10d nails. Cut four supports each from a 2×4×120-in. piece. Save the scraps. As you install these supports, note their location on the plan for proper positioning of shelves.

Materials List **Potting Shed**	
Pcs	**Size and description**
2	4×4×120″ lumber
1	4×4×96″ lumber
5	2×6×72″ lumber
6	2×4×120″ lumber
1	2×4×96″ lumber
8	2×4×72″ lumber
1	1×8×72″ lumber
14	1×4×72″ lumber
2	48×96×⅜″ T-111 plywood siding

Miscellaneous:
21 sq. ft. roofing materials:
      sheathing plywood
      15 lb. felt
      asphalt or fiberglass shingles
Ridge and eave drip
Concrete blocks (base)

Fasteners:
8d, 10d and 12d galvanized nails
Galvanized roofing nails
¼×3″ galvanized lag screws

Tools:
Circular or crosscut saw, hammer, ½″ socket wrench, ¼″ drill, a square and a level

Finishing the potting shed.

Next, assemble the 2×4 interior frame. Cut six more 2×4×24½-in. supports from the 120 in. lengths. Cut two rear posts 2×4×104½-in. long with an angle cut at the top to match the 4×4 posts. Also, cut a notch at the top to receive the 2×6 cross brace.

Make the 2×4 front posts by cutting a 72 in. length in half. Build two frames by nailing the front and rear 2×4 posts together, each with three supports. Use 10d nails and construction adhesive.

From scrap material, cut 2×4×3½-in. cleats and nail them into place on the inner frame assemblies, as shown. Then cut 2×4 cleats for the upper 1×8 shelf, locate them on the 2×4 rear posts and nail them into place. Also attach two cleats to the 4×4 rear posts using 10d nails.

Attach the 2×4 interior frame by driving 10d nails through the front 2×6s into the front 2×4 posts. Make sure the frame remains level and square.

Cut a 2×6×62-in. piece and install it across the top of the 2×4 rear posts using 10d nails. Toenail the ends to the 4×4 corner posts.

Cut two pieces of plywood siding 48×57-in., then nail them to the rear of the 4×4 posts and

2×4 frames with 8d nails. Position the panels horizontally with the pattern facing the front.

Next cut six 2×4×69-in. shelves and attach them to the shelf supports using 10d nails and construction adhesive. Cut one of the 2×4s to fit between the rear posts and nail it to cleats and supports installed earlier.

Install the 1×4 storage shelves in the same manner. Then attach the 1×8 shelf to the 2×4 cleats using 10d nails, making sure you notch appropriate shelves to fit around the 2×4 rear posts.

Then begin the roof. Cut four pairs of 2×4 rafters and braces according to the plan. Attach both to frame posts using lag screws and construction adhesive. Join the rafter to the brace with a 2×4 splice plate made from scrap material. Use 10d nails.

Attach the ½-in. sheathing plywood to the rafters using 8d nails.

Install roofing felt and shingles. Attach the eave drip across the rafter ends and the metal ridge across the joint of the roof with the rear wall panel.

Once you're done, coat your new potting shed with a water-repellent sealer.

7 Gazebos and Decorative Structures

Gazebos range in design from simple units just large enough for a rocking chair to elaborate shade pavilions. There are other gazebo plans in Volume 27 of your *Popular Mechanics Do-it-Yourself Encyclopedia*. You'll also want to review the material about outdoor construction in Chapter 1 of this book before you try any of the projects given here.

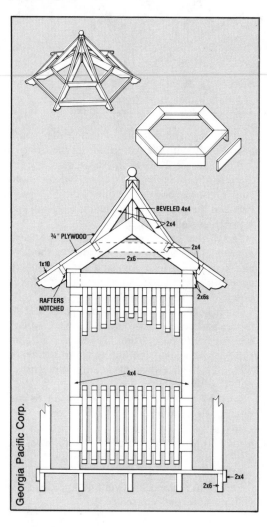

BEVELED 4x4
2x4
¾" PLYWOOD
2x4
1x10
2x6
2x6s
RAFTERS NOTCHED
4x4
2x4
2x6

Georgia Pacific Corp.

Planning Your Gazebo

Gazebos require space, which is why they became nearly extinct as home lot sizes became smaller over the years. Ten by 14 ft. is the ideal space to allow for most gazebos. You may decide to increase this somewhat to allow for planting shade trees nearby or constructing a path to your structure. The most popular size is an 8-ft.-wide octagon.

The gazebo is simple to construct if you do the job one step at a time. The foundation can be of blocks on pads, piers, poured concrete or pressure-treated wood. Construct a frame on your foundation, then install the plywood flooring. Place upright posts around the perimeter and cross-frame with stringers between them. Next, install the roof rafters, then cover them with lath, wood or asphalt shingles. You can finish the walls with plastic screening, glass, textured plywood, lattice, paneling or leave the walls open.

Square Gazebo

The square gazebo is more than just an outdoor shelter. It functions as a backyard retreat for warm summer afternoons, casual dining, or a neighborhood meeting house. This gazebo plan includes several options that you can use to dress up your structure. It's a flexible design that you can tailor to fit your yard's personality. You can also screen the sections for protection against insects.

The first step in building your square gazebo is determining its exact location. Use stakes, line and level to locate the positions of concrete footings. Excavate an area 18×27×6-in. deep for each footing. Pour the footings and install 4×4 post anchor bases. Then allow sufficient time for concrete to set before continuing.

Position pairs of 4×4×120-in. posts in the anchor bases at the corners. Attach the bases to posts using 12d nails. Attach the front 2×6×168-in. beam so that the top edge of the beam is 5½ in. from the top of the 4×4 posts for stability.

Install the two 2×6×168-in. end ceiling joists with a 3½-in. overhang. They should fit between the 4×4 posts and rest on the 2×6 beams. Toenail the joists into the posts using 12d nails. Verify that the frame has remained level and square.

Install the two 2×8×168-in. end beams in the same manner with the top edge of the beam 1 in. below the finished deck surface. Toenail the beams to the posts using 12d nails. Trim overhang to 3½ in. beyond the posts.

Build two triple 2×8×134-in. beams with 2×2 ledger (bottom inside edge) to support the floor deck. Use 10d nails and construction adhesive. Install beams to the inside of the front and rear 4×4 posts making sure the top edge is flush with the top of the 2×8 beams. Fasten with 12d nails and construction adhesive. Verify square and level.

To complete the floor framing, install eight 2×8 floor joists 16-in. o.c. Notch each to rest on the 2×2 ledger. Toenail them to the 2×8 beams using 12d nails. Then add 2×8 bridging along the centerline of the floor joist span with 10d nails.

Install the 1×6 deck boards bark side up on the floor joists. Start them flush with one 2×8 end beam and trim the opposite ends flush with the other end beam when done.

Attach a 2×4 ledger to the 2×8 floor beams on all four sides except at the door opening. Position the top of the 2×4 ledger 1½ in. below the deck surface to support privacy screen wall sections.

Install the 2×4 bench supports on the two sides. Attach a 2×4 between the 4×4 posts so that the top edge is 14½ in. above the deck surface. Toenail them to the posts using 10d nails.

Build the side wall privacy screens by first constructing a 2×4 frame to fit between the 4×4 corner posts, the 2×6 end ceiling joists and the 2×4 ledger installed earlier. Equally divide the screen width into thirds and install 2×4 vertical supports at these locations. Mark 30 in. from the top of the screen frame and attach 2×4 horizontals at this mark, toenailing with 10d nails. Then cut 2×2s to fit between the horizontals, equally spacing nine 2×2s 4½-in. o.c. between the 2×4 verticals (see plan). Align with the inside of the 2×4 frame. Using the same spacing and alignment, attach 2×2×15-in. pieces to the bottom 2×4 frame member. Lift the wall section into place between the 4×4 posts and nail the 2×2s at the bottom to the outside of the bench support. Nail the 2×4 wall frame to the posts and ledger with 10d nails.

Square gazebo construction details.

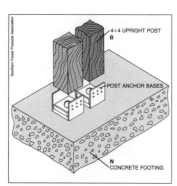

Detail showing how to anchor posts to foundation.

Detail showing post and beam construction.

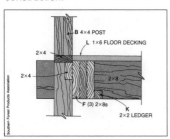

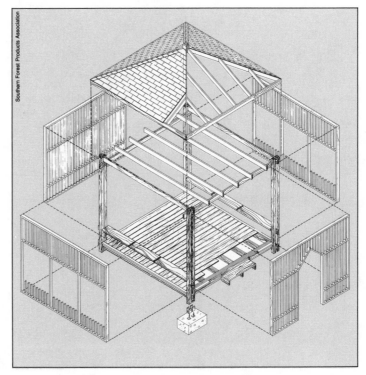

Cut 2×12 benches to fit between the 2×4 privacy screen verticals. Then cut two bench braces per seat out of 2×8 scrap. Install the bench and braces using 10d nails.

Construct the rear screen section with the same kind of 2×4 frame. Add 2×4 horizontals between the verticals at a level even with the benches. Equally space 2×2s within all openings, 4½-in. o.c. as shown in the plan. Use 10d nails to fasten. Lift the wall into position between the rear posts and attach to the 2×4 frame with 10d nails.

Construct the front wall screen in the same way except that you will include a 36×84-in. opening for a door. The opening can be square or pointed. Frame the door with 2×4 material. Attach the completed wall section to the posts and ledger using 10d nails.

To complete the roof framing, install five 2×6×168-in. ceiling joists to rest on the 2×6 beams front and rear. Evenly space the joists approximately 23-in. o.c. Taper at least 2 in. off the top and corners of the 6×6 piece for use as a roof peak. Use the 2×6×120-in. material for all rafters. Cut four 2×6s to serve as ridge rafters following the roof slope. Add center rafters square to each side of the 6×6 peak, then intermediate rafters in line with the ceiling joists.

Trim front and rear rafters 1½ in. short of the ceiling joist ends. Side rafters extend 3½ in. beyond the outside face of the 4×4 posts. Install 2×6×168-in. roof fascia to all rafter ends using 10d nails.

Complete the roof by nailing ¾-in. exterior plywood sheathing to all rafters with 8d nails.

Materials List Square Gazebo		
Key	**Pcs**	**Size and description**
A	1	6×6×24″ lumber
B	8	4×4×120″ lumber
C	2	2×12×144″ lumber
D	1	2×12×96″ lumber
E	2	2×8×168″ lumber
F	16	2×8×144″ lumber
G	15	2×6×168″ lumber
H	16	2×6×120″ lumber
J	30	2×4×144″ lumber
K	80	2×2×96″ lumber
L	26	1×6×144″ lumber
M	8	48×96×¾″ plywood (roof sheathing)
N	4	18×27×6″ concrete (footings)
P	160 sq. ft. 15 lb. felt (roofing)		
Q	160 sq. ft. roofing shingles		

Fasteners:
8d, 10d, 12d, 16d galvanized nails
4×4″ post anchor bases
Roofing nails

Tools:
Circular or crosscut saw, hammer, stakes, line, level, square, shovel, carpenter's tape and a ladder

Plans for a square gazebo frame.

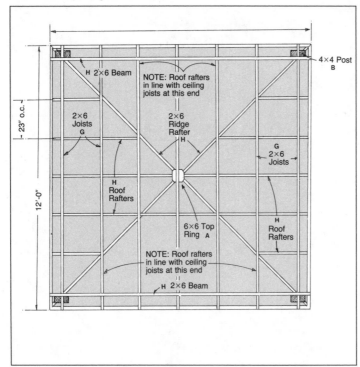

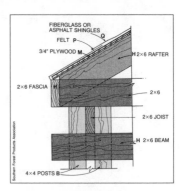

Detail showing cap construction.

Detail showing joist and ledger.

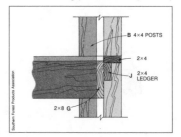

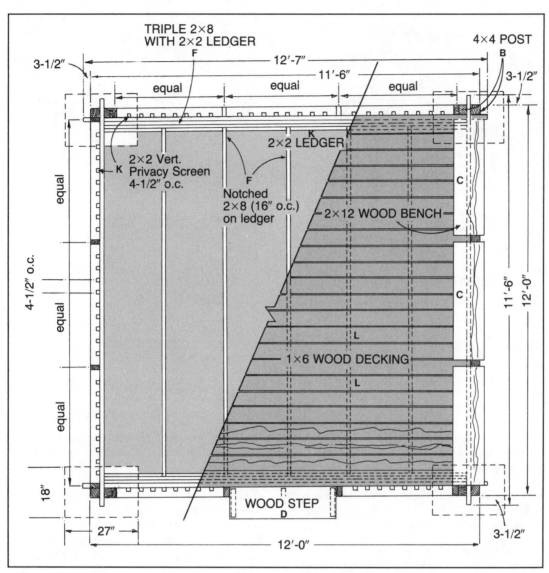

TRIPLE 2×8
WITH 2×2 LEDGER
F

4×4 POST
B

3-1/2"

12'-7"

11'-6"

3-1/2"

equal

equal

equal

2×2 LEDGER
K

2×2 Vert.
K Privacy Screen
4-1/2" o.c.

F
Notched
2×8 (16" o.c.)
on ledger

2×12 WOOD BENCH

C

equal

4-1/2" o.c.

11'-6"

12'-0"

C

equal

1×6 WOOD DECKING

L

L

equal

18"

WOOD STEP
D

3-1/2"

27"

12'-0"

Floor plan for installing wood decking over square gazebo frame.

Attached Gazebo

You can extend your living space to the out-doors while controlling insects with an attached square gazebo.

The floor can be an existing patio or a specially poured slab. If you're going to use an existing patio, put down sole plates on a bed of mastic and secure then with case-hardened nails. If it's a new slab, prepare the sole plate by setting anchor bolts in the concrete when it is poured. In either case, an alternative method is to secure posts with ready-made post anchors. Like anchor bolts, they are best set in fresh concrete. Attaching to an existing slab will call for drilling holes with a carbide-tipped masonry bit and using expansion sleeves and lag screws.

Using post anchors allows you to eliminate the sole plate if you wish.

Install framed screens secured with stops between posts for easy replacement or repair. You can purchase ready-made screen doors available in 36 in. widths or make your own. The screens don't have to be the full height of the wall. You can fill in part way up between posts with 2×4-in. sills and cripple studs covered with plywood siding.

The roof of your attached gazebo can be a translucent material like fiberglass or it can be the traditional shingles-over-plywood roof system. You can also install lath in a lattice design, depending on local weather conditions.

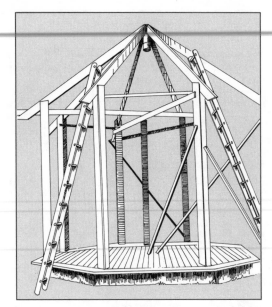

Octagon gazebo frame.

Hexagon Gazebo

Here's a unique version of the popular hexagon gazebo that can be constructed of either pressure-treated lumber, redwood or cedar. This hexagon, or six-sided gazebo measures 8 ft. from any two parallel sides. The plans shown here for an 8-sided (octagon) gazebo show basically the same construction details.

You can substitute 1× or 2× lumber for the tongue-and-groove flooring if you desire. Support the floor boards with three 2×6 joists. Nail a skirt of 2×4s to the perimeter. Toenail six 4×4×96-in. posts to the floor boards.

Floor framing detail for octagon gazebo.

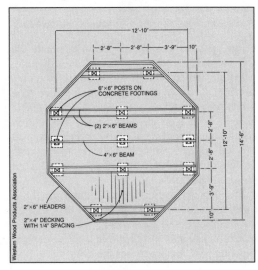

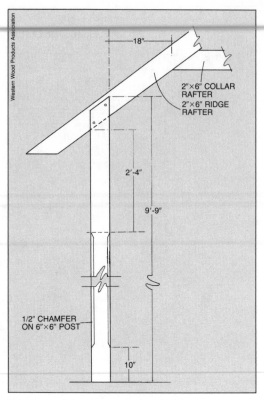

Octagon gazebo post and rafter detail.

Measure the space between the posts and assemble the sections of railings and top trim to fit: cross-pieces of the railings are 2×4s, top trim is of 2×4s and 2×2s. The vertical slats are made of 2×2s that have been angle-cut as shown. Toenail these sections into place.

The four posts on the two open sides of the gazebo are trimmed with 2×6s. Also note the little shelf shown on the far side of the gazebo, constructed from a 2×4 or 2×6.

Angle-cut and bevel the 2×6s that form the top plate which runs around the top of the gazebo. Nail the horizontal 2×6s to the vertical ones as shown, forming what looks like giant-size molding. Nail these pieces to the posts.

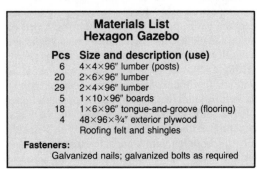

Materials List Hexagon Gazebo	
Pcs	**Size and description (use)**
6	4×4×96″ lumber (posts)
20	2×6×96″ lumber
29	2×4×96″ lumber
5	1×10×96″ boards
18	1×6×96″ tongue-and-groove (flooring)
4	48×96×¾″ exterior plywood Roofing felt and shingles

Fasteners:
Galvanized nails; galvanized bolts as required

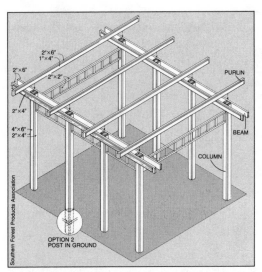

Trellis can become a decorative outdoor structure for afternoon relaxation.

Make the lower rafters of 2×6s and notch them to accommodate the 2×6s of the top plate. This section of roof has a pitch of 10 in 12 (10-inch rise for every 12 inches of span). Nail the twelve beams to the rafters. Then make the upper rafters for a pitch of 17 in 12. Toenail these rafters to the lower ones. Insert a spike made from two laminated and beveled 2×6s into the hole bordered by the ends of the upper and lower rafters. Nail it in place.

Finally, cover the rafters with sheathing made of 1×10s and ¾-in. exterior-grade plywood. Top the sheathing with roofing felt and roofing material (cedar shakes offer a rustic look).

Roof plan for octagon gazebo.

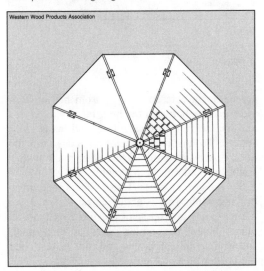

Trellis

With simple modifications, a trellis can serve as a frame for climbing vines and hanging plants, as a shade screen or as the base for a deck roof. This plan is for a 14×16 ft. trellis installed over a deck. You can, however, modify the plan to match nearly any size area. You can sink the columns 36 in. into the ground using concrete, incorporate it into your deck by connecting columns with deck posts and beams, or attach it on two sides to your house or other permanent structure.

First, cut smaller materials from larger. Cut 46 pieces 9-in. long from ten of the 2×2s. Cut 8 pieces 20 in. long from three of the 1×4s.

Fabricate the columns by centering a 2×4×144-in. piece on the wide dimension of each 4×6-in. timber; nail into place using 12d nails. Then fabricate purlins by centering 1×4-in. pieces along the four 2×6×168-in. lumber. Use two 1×4×72-in. pieces and one 20-in. piece on each side of a 2×6. Attach the 1×4s using 6d nails and construction adhesive.

Locate and mark column location on 2×6×192-in. beam members, 48 in. o.c. Attach the beams to both sides of the columns using 12d nails and construction adhesive. Center the 2×4×192-in. pieces on the beams and attach them using 8d nails and construction adhesive.

Set up the column/beam assemblies 120 in. on center. Attach purlins to the center of the columns, toenailing the purlins into columns using 16d nails and construction adhesive. Ends of the purlins should extend beyond the column centerline by 24 in., as the beam ends.

Complete trim assemblies between columns with 2×2s, 8d nails and construction adhesive. Make exact measurements between the beams and evenly space 11 2×2s across the two 10-ft. spans. Space 4 2×2s across the shorter spans of approximately 42 inches.

Finally, attach trim assemblies between beams using 8d nails and construction adhesive.

Materials List Trellis	
Pcs	**Size and description**
8	4×6×144″ lumber*
4	2×6×192″ lumber
4	2×6×168″ lumber
4	2×4×192″ lumber
16	2×4×144″ lumber*
4	2×2×120″ lumber
22	2×2×48″ lumber
19	1×4×72″ lumber
* = shorten by 24 in. if columns will be sunk in the ground	

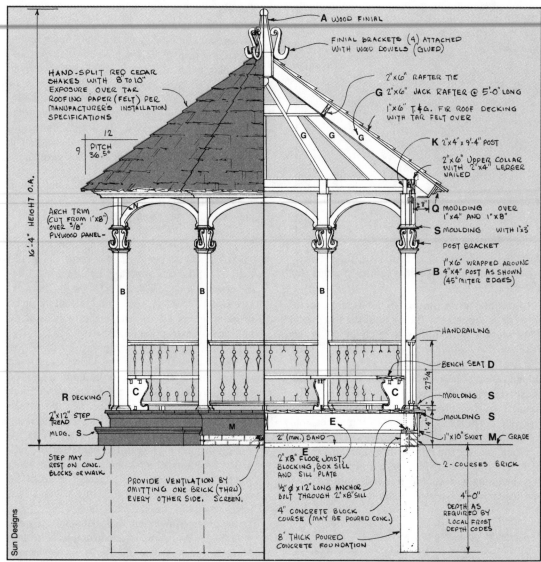

A WOOD FINIAL

FINIAL BRACKETS (4) ATTACHED WITH WOOD DOWELS (GLUED)

2"x6" RAFTER TIE

G 2"x6" JACK RAFTER @ 5'-0" LONG

1"x6" T.&G. FIR ROOF DECKING WITH TAR FELT OVER

K 2"x4" x 9'-4" POST

2"x6" UPPER COLLAR WITH 2"x4" LEDGER NAILED

Q MOULDING OVER 1"x4" AND 1"x8"

S MOULDING WITH 1"x3"

POST BRACKET

B 1"x6" WRAPPED AROUND 4"x4" POST AS SHOWN (45° MITER EDGES)

HAND-SPLIT RED CEDAR SHAKES WITH 8 TO 10" EXPOSURE OVER TAR ROOFING PAPER (FELT) PER MANUFACTURER'S INSTALLATION SPECIFICATIONS

12 / 9 PITCH 36.5°

16'-4" HEIGHT O.A.

ARCH TRIM (CUT FROM 1"x8") OVER 5/8" PLYWOOD PANEL

HANDRAILING

BENCH SEAT D

27 3/4"

MOULDING S

MOULDING S

1"x10" SKIRT M GRADE

2-COURSES BRICK

R DECKING

2"x12" STEP TREAD

MLDG. S

STEP MAY REST ON CONC. BLOCKS OR WALK

PROVIDE VENTILATION BY OMITTING ONE BRICK (THRU) EVERY OTHER SIDE. SCREEN.

M

E

2' (MIN.) SAND

E

2"x8" FLOOR JOIST BLOCKING, BOX SILL AND SILL PLATE

1/2" Ø x12" LONG ANCHOR BOLT THROUGH 2"x8" SILL

4" CONCRETE BLOCK COURSE (MAY BE POURED CONC.)

8" THICK POURED CONCRETE FOUNDATION

4'-0" DEPTH AS REQUIRED BY LOCAL FROST DEPTH CODES

Sun Designs

Construction details for ornate Tiffany gazebo.

Tiffany Gazebo

If you're an ambitious and skilled do-it-your-selfer, you may want to build this old-fashioned gazebo with a brick base and ornate gingerbread trim.

Constructing the Tiffany gazebo is similar to building the hexagon gazebo. First, mark out the area on which you will build. Use a carpenter's level and tape to establish a level point for your foundation. Drive wood stakes at the corners.

Install joists and floor framing. Before nailing the deck, cover the floor joists with aluminum

screen so insects can't enter from below. Provide spacing between the floor boards to let dirt and water run through. Use 16d nails as a spacer. To ensure a straight cut edge, run the deck boards past the edges, then mark with a chalk line and cut them evenly.

Set the corner posts. Use 2×4s as temporary bracing while you establish corners. When the corner posts are set, nail the top 2×4 plate in place. Install the center rafter or finial post. Install the top wall plates and roof rafters over the corner posts for maximum support.

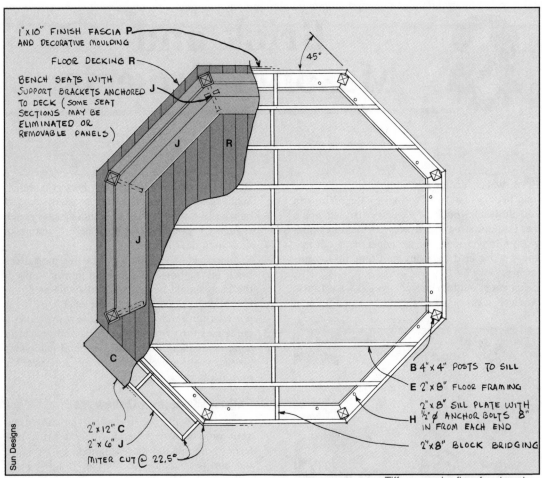

1" x 10" FINISH FASCIA **P** AND DECORATIVE MOULDING

FLOOR DECKING **R**

BENCH SEATS WITH SUPPORT BRACKETS ANCHORED **J** TO DECK (SOME SEAT SECTIONS MAY BE ELIMINATED OR REMOVABLE PANELS)

45°

J

R

J

J

C

2" x 12" **C**
2" x 6" **J**
MITER CUT @ 22.5°

B 4" x 4" POSTS TO SILL

E 2" x 8" FLOOR FRAMING

H 2" x 8" SILL PLATE WITH ½" ø ANCHOR BOLTS 8" IN FROM EACH END

2" x 8" BLOCK BRIDGING

Sun Designs

Tiffany gazebo floor framing plan.

Materials List Tiffany Gazebo

Key	Pcs	Size and description (use)	Key	Pcs	Size and description (use)
A	1	8×8″ turned finial	U	7	1×1×96″ lumber (glazing stop)
B	8	4×4×104″ lumber (posts)	V	80	¼×2×120″ lumber (lattice)
C	1	2×12×144″ lumber (seat supports)	W	11	48×96×½″ CDX plywood (sheathing)
D	3	2×8×120″ lumber (seat boards)			
E	10	2×8×120″ lumber (floor joists)	**Miscellaneous:**		
F	4	2×8×120″ lumber (collar)			288 sq. ft. roofing felt
G	23	2×6×144″ lumber (rafters)			288 sq. ft. shingles or shakes
H	4	2×6×120″ lumber (plate)			7 pcs. molding (fascia trim)
J	3	2×6×120″ lumber (seat boards)			8 stained glass panels
K	6	2×4×120″ lumber (rail cap & bottom)			4 cubic yards 3000 PSI Concrete (foundation)
L	4	2×4×120″ lumber (ledger)			32 4″ concrete blocks
M	4	1×10×120″ lumber (skirt)			200 common bricks
N	7	1×8×96″ lumber (glazing frame)			
P	7	1×8×96″ lumber (fascia board)	**Fasteners:**		
Q	4	Cove molding			½×8″ anchor bolts
R	33	1×4×144″ tongue & groove (decking)			¼×6″ lag screws
S	1	1×3×144″ lumber (column base trim)			Fastener clips (rafters to collar)
T	8	1×2½×96″ lumber (glazing trim)			L-clips (bench seat to ground)
					Common galvanized nails

Brick and Masonry Projects

Brick walks, driveways, steps and walls have long been a feature of formal estates. You can add the same touch of elegance to your home and outdoor structure project. Mortarless brick-work removes many of the concerns about masonry work held by many first-time do-it-your-selfers.

For most outdoor projects you'll want to use paving bricks or "pavers" that are rated SW and stand up under severe weather conditions. While other types of bricks can be used, it would be wise to review the recommended uses of each type in Chapter 1 of this book before you make your final decision.

A concrete foundation is best for mortarless brick installations. Because no mortar is used, the base should be as level and stable as possible. Make sure you have a slope of at least ¼-in. per foot for good drainage. Review the general guidelines for working with brick and mortar in Chapter 1, then follow these general guidelines given by the Brick Institute of America for mortarless brick projects.

Patios, Walks and Driveways

For patios, walks or driveways you can design your project with several different brick patterns. Some of the more common patterns are the herringbone, basket weave, running bond and stack bond.

Prepare the Area. Outline the area of your walk, driveway or patio with stakes and string. Excavate about 1-inch deeper than the thickness of the brick you are using. Extend the excavation about 2 or 3 inches beyond the planned finished boundary.

Brick walkways are an easy mortarless brick project. Restraining brick on sides keep walk from shifting.

Paving brick designs can be quite varied. The easiest are the **basket weave** and **running** designs.

Concrete foundation over a bed of gravel and sand is best for mortarless brick installations.

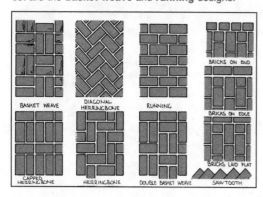

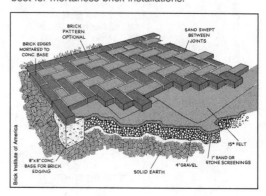

Outline with stakes and string. Excavate to a depth of about 1-in. more than the thickness of the brick.

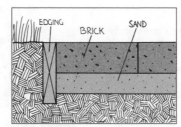

Redwood or pressure-treated lumber outlines the area and serves as a stop to keep the brick in place.

Fill area with sand or stone screenings and level with screed board (notch end to brick thickness).

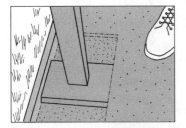

Moisten sand with mist from garden hose them compact with wooden tamper (or use a lawn roller) until base is smooth.

Use string as guides to set brick square. Lay brick according to pattern selected. Tap bricks in place.

Spread sand over brick and sweep into cracks to lock brick into position. Repeat sand sweeping until stabilized.

Install Borders. Borders are made by framing the edges with redwood 2×4s or pressure-treated lumber. Secure firmly with treated stakes, driven below grade and nailed to the border. Install forms two sides in a temporary position 2 to 3 inches beyond the stringline at 4- to 5-ft. intervals to serve as leveling guides.

Level the Sand Fill. Fill the area with sand or stone screenings. A gravel base about 4-in. deep under a layer of 1-in. stone screenings is the best alternative to a concrete base. A 1-in. or 2-in. sand cushion is an economical but less durable choice. Level the sand with a wooden screed board (notch the ends to the thickness of the paver brick). Moisten the sand with a light mist from a garden hose and compact with a wooden tamper or lawn roller. Add more sand, mist and screed the area again until it is smooth and well compacted.

Laying the Brick. Cover the sand with 15-lb. roofing felt before laying your brick; this will prevent the "greening" effect caused by algae. It also makes the bricklaying process easier.

Start at one corner and lay one run of brick along each of two permanent borders. These bricks should be laid flat with the longest dimension horizontal and the face parallel to the edge. This restraining edge is necessary because mortarless brick tend to shift at the edges. No restraining is necessary where paving can be abutted to existing curbs or structures. Bricks should fit snugly or hand-tight. Stay outside the framework as you work to avoid disturbing the sand bed

Maintain Brick Alignment. With the perimeter brick for reference, maintain brick alignment by working toward string or chalk lines forming 2- to 3-ft. square sections. Use a mason's trowel, screwdriver or wide-bladed putty knife to adjust brick spacing. Reposition the two temporary edge forms as permanent boarders. Secure firmly with wood stakes driven below grade and nailed to border. Backfill as needed.

Stabilize the Brick. Inspect the entire area after all bricks are laid. Make final adjustments in brick heights and joint alignments. Then sweep sand into all joints to lock brick into position. You may have to repeat the sand-sweeping operation every 2 or 3 days until the bricks are fully stabilized.

Lawn Edging and Stepping Stones

Brick edging and stepping stones are the easiest of all brick projects.

Stepping Stones. Stepping stones can be made from decorative squares of brick. For each stepping stone, excavate a square hole 4-in. deep and large enough to accommodate a 17½-in. (outside dimensions) frame of redwood plank. Place the stepping-stone units about 4-in. apart. Position the frame in the excavation so that its top is level with the grass line. Mix 1 part cement to 3 parts sand and spread about 1 in. to 1½ in. of this mixture, dry, in the hole. Tamp it down; add more if needed to be sure it is level with the frame. Lay the bricks on the cushion in the pattern shown; make sure they are flush with the top of the frame.

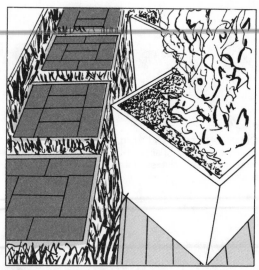

Brick stepping stones you can build.

Make forms for each stepping stone from redwood or pressure-treated lumber.

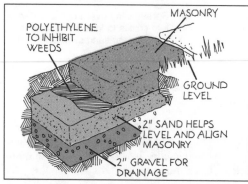

Set brick on 2-in. layer of sand, for drainage, and a 2-in. base of gravel. This makes realigning easier.

Brick edging around lawn and garden areas.

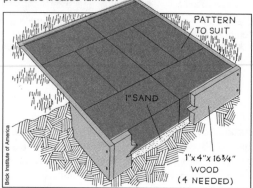

Brick Edging. Brick edging around lawn and garden areas is both attractive and functional. An almost endless variety of earthy brick colors will enhance your greenery and simplify mowing and trimming chores.

With a flat-bladed spade, dig up the sod about 4-in. deep where you want the edging. Make a continuous cut about 10-in. wide. Put down a layer of sand and place the bricks flat on it. Slight curves may be made by fanning the bricks slightly; sharper curves will call for cutting wedge-shaped bricks. When the job is finished, sweep sand between the bricks and in the trench between the brick edges and the sod.

Changes in weather may make the brick edging rise and fall. You can fix this problem easily be removing the affected units and smoothing out the gravel and sand underneath.

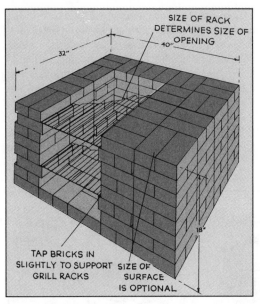

Retaining Wall

Brick retaining walls protect your property while enhancing its appearance. When a cut is made in a hillside, escaping moisture will eventually erode the hill. Retaining walls prevent this erosion by holding moisture in the ground.

A retaining wall is an ambitious project and calls for particularly good workmanship. Remember to comply with local building codes. This wall is to be built no more than 3-ft. high. Study the diagram and refer to it often as you work.

Dig the excavation as indicated. Use some loose brick to lay the bottom reinforcing bars on. Wire the vertical bar to the bottom bar and prop it in place. Insert the remaining bars in the top of the footing as you pour the concrete. Let the concrete footing season for at least a week.

Lay up the brick, using your best workmanship and shoved joints. Insert prefabricated steel joint reinforcement where indicated. Some bricks must be cut so you can insert "weep holes" of 1-in.-dia. plastic tubing every 4 ft. along the wall as shown. A "French drain" of gravel should be placed (as shown) behind the wall down to the weep hole.

Before capping the wall with a solid row of bricks laid on edge, pour grout in the gap between the brick to bond the reinforcing bars. *Grout* is mortar to which you add water until it is thin enough to pour.

When the wall is completed, brush an asphalt coating on the back side of the wall next to the earth on the hill to make it watertight.

Mortarless Barbecue

You should be able to build this barbecue in a couple of hours. Bear in mind one important requirement of mortarless brick work: the site you select must be absolutely level and stable. A concrete slab is best.

Buy your grill racks first; sometimes availability of certain sizes is limited. You can adjust the construction of the barbecue to the size grill racks you buy. You'll need a 2-ft. carpenter's level and about 236 bricks each measuring $3\frac{3}{4} \times 2\frac{1}{4} \times 8$-inch for the barbecue shown.

As you follow the pattern shown, be careful to tap the bricks that support the grill racks before going on to the adjacent optional work surface. The brick units supporting the grill racks should be tapped in with a 2×4 and a hammer. Lay the 2×4 edgewise as you tap the bricks in.

Mortarless barbecue is built in a couple of hours.

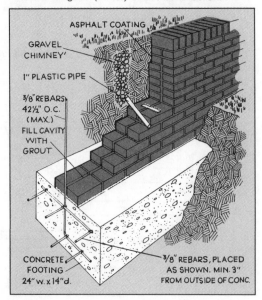

Brick retaining wall *(above)* keeps water from eroding hillsides. Diagram *(below)* details construction.

Outdoor Fireplace

A large brick outdoor fireplace has been a long-time backyard favorite. While it requires more time and money to construct than other backyard projects, it can offer many years of enjoyment and, perhaps, even increase the value of your home.

The size and depth for the excavation, fill, and foundation are shown in the foundation detail in the drawing.

Lay out the first course of brick. Fill the cavity in the center with gravel and mortar, and then lay one more course. Lay fire bricks along the bottom of the fireplace opening, bringing them flush with the third course of bricks along the front of the opening. Extend the two side walls and back 12 in. up from the bottom of the opening, lining them with fire brick.

Twelve inches from the base, the fire brick back begins to slope forward, while the side

Elevation and plan section for brick fireplace.

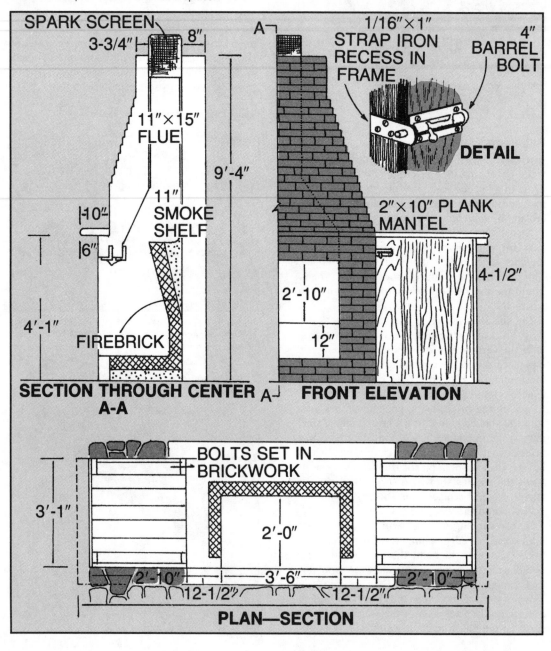

walls and common brick portion of the back wall continue upward in a straight line. The inside surface of the back wall slopes forward until it is 4 ft. from the fireplace foundation. It is also 11 inches out from the common bricks of the back wall, forming a throat 8×42-inches. Fill the space between the fire bricks and the common bricks with small stones and mortar. You can save time and trouble by making a rough wood pattern or form for the fire bricks to follow.

Next, bring the side walls up 34 in. from the bottom of the fireplace opening and then install two angle irons—measuring 3×4×¼×54-in.—between these side walls to support the front breast of the fireplace. The back of the fireplace should be carried up so that the 11-in. wide smoke shelf can be formed. Make this shelf just as flat as you can get it.

The rest of the masonry is all common brick. No more fire brick will be required. At the point

Construction details for brick fireplace.

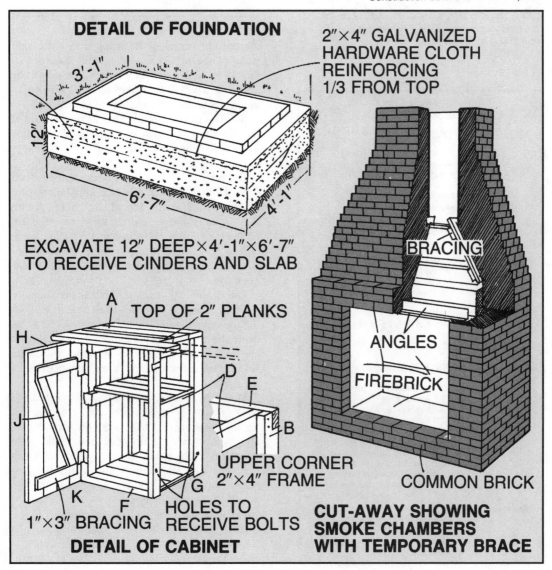

DETAIL OF FOUNDATION

3'-1"

2"×4" GALVANIZED HARDWARE CLOTH REINFORCING 1/3 FROM TOP

12"

6'-7"

4'-1"

EXCAVATE 12" DEEP×4'-1"×6'-7" TO RECEIVE CINDERS AND SLAB

BRACING

A TOP OF 2" PLANKS

H

D

E

J

B

K F G

UPPER CORNER 2"×4" FRAME

1"×3" BRACING

HOLES TO RECEIVE BOLTS

DETAIL OF CABINET

ANGLES

FIREBRICK

COMMON BRICK

CUT-AWAY SHOWING SMOKE CHAMBERS WITH TEMPORARY BRACE

This outdoor fireplace will serve summer cooking and entertaining needs for many years.

Building With Brick

You'll find additional help for building with brick and mortar in Chapter 1 of this book. For all brick and mortar projects shown in this chapter, you'll have to be sure to use shoved joints when laying brick and to tool the joints for proper moisture sealing.

Materials List
Outdoor Fireplace
FOUNDATION

Pcs	Size and description (use)
14 cubic feet	cinder or gravel fill
2¾ bags	cement
⅖ cubic yards	gravel or
14 cubic feet	ready-mixed concrete
⅕ cubic yard	sand

FIREPLACE

Pcs	Size and description (use)
5 bags	cement
4 bags	hydrated lime
1 cubic yard	sand or
25 cubic feet	ready-mixed mortar
1700	common bricks
200	fire bricks
3 lb.	fireclay (add 25% Portland cement)
2	angle irons 3×4×¼×54″
1	mantle 2×10″×12′

CABINETS (two)

Key	Pcs	Size and description (use)
A	8	2×8×34″ lumber (top)
B	8	2×4×49″ lumber (frame)
C	2	2×4×31″ lumber (back frame)
D	8	2×4×35½″ lumber (cross members)
E	2	2×4×34″ lumber (back frame)
F	4	2×4×33¾″ lumber (bottom frame)
G	4	2×4×22¾″ lumber (bottom frame)
H	1	1×8×49″ lumber (siding, shelves)
J	2	1×3×38″ lumber (door bracing)
K	4	1×3×30″ lumber (door bracing)

Fasteners:

8	¼×6″ carriage bolts, nuts, washer
4	3″ butt hinges
2	4″ barrel bolts
2	1/16×1″ strap irons

where you installed the angle irons, the side walls of the fireplace start coming together so that 18 in. above the smoke shelf, the side walls are 15 in. apart. This makes an 11×15-in. opening. Smooth the side walls with mortar.

Build up three courses of bricks on the front of the fireplace and support them with the angle irons. After the third course, form a 4-in. recess in the front to carry a 10-in. mantle.

The brick work for the chimney should extend 9 ft., 4 in. above the fireplace foundation. Cap off the bricks at the top of the chimney with mortar and slope the mortar so water will drain off the masonry. Let the masonry harden a week before removing the wood forms from the inside, and then give it another week before building a fire.

The cabinets on each side of the fireplace are 37 in. deep and 34 in. wide. Their height, without the top covering of 2-in. planks, should be 49 in. from the fireplace foundation. These cabinets are fastened to the fireplace masonry with bolts set into the mortar joints during construction of the fireplace.

Make the cabinets with a framework of 2×4s covered with 1- and 2-in. boards. Don't install the top covering of 2×8 boards until the cabinets are in place and you have fastened the fireplace mantle in position. The mantle extends out along the edge of each cabinet and forms the first board of the top. After this is in place, you can install the remaining boards.

Because the cabinets will be exposed to the weather, use non-corrosive hardware, such as brass, for bolt, striker and hinges. You can cover the cabinets with several coats of varnish.

Barbecue pit *(right)* can be made of brick or stone. Plans *(below)* show construction details.

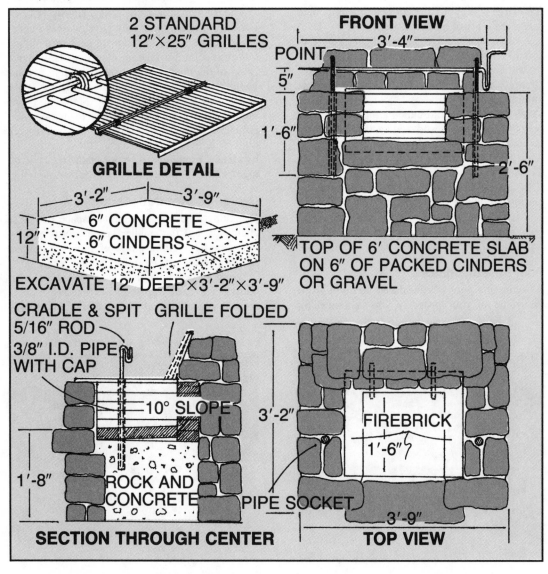

2 STANDARD 12″×25″ GRILLES

FRONT VIEW

3′-4″

POINT

5″

1′-6″

2′-6″

GRILLE DETAIL

3′-2″   3′-9″

6″ CONCRETE
6″ CINDERS
12″

EXCAVATE 12″ DEEP×3′-2″×3′-9″

TOP OF 6′ CONCRETE SLAB ON 6″ OF PACKED CINDERS OR GRAVEL

CRADLE & SPIT   GRILLE FOLDED
5/16″ ROD
3/8″ I.D. PIPE WITH CAP

10° SLOPE

3′-2″

FIREBRICK
1′-6″

1′-8″

ROCK AND CONCRETE

PIPE SOCKET

3′-9″

SECTION THROUGH CENTER   **TOP VIEW**

9 Swimming Pools and Spas

Innovative products, creative designs and customized plans allow people with small or unusually shaped spaces to relax, entertain and exercise in their own outdoor swimming pool, spa or hot tub. Even if you don't have the yard space for a large pool, you can choose a smaller pool to make the most of a limited area.

A swimming pool is an excellent project to test all your skills in outdoor construction. Even if you don't actually dig the hole and pour the concrete yourself, you can save a considerable amount of money and add your own personal touch by planning and building the decking and poolside structures, and adding the warmth of landscaping yourself. You'll find many helpful poolside structure projects in Volume 23 of your *Popular Mechanics Do-it-Yourself Encyclopedia*.

In this chapter you'll find many tips from the National Pool and Spa Institute that will help you design and plan a pool or spa that will fit not only your backyard space, but your family's recreational preferences as well.

Pool Responsibilities

A swimming pool is considered an addition to the value of your property and in almost all localities, building a pool is tightly controlled by local building and zoning codes. Find out what restrictions your community places on building and using backyard pools before you make any investment in its planning or construction.

You should also know what liability restrictions a swimming pool may have on your homeowner's insurance. The high diving board has all but disappeared from community pools in many areas of the country because of rapidly growing liability insurance costs. Some municipal pools have even closed completely. Many of these increased insurance costs apply to homeowner policies as well. It's best to find out before you dig! You may discover that the increase in insurance premiums is more than the cost of membership in a neighborhood swimming pool.

Design Considerations

Designing a pool to fit a limited space can be a challenge, but the smaller spaces actually provide a more definite framework in which to plan and can result in a more intimate setting.

Work with a builder to help you plan your limited pool area with the right amount of deck area. If you want decking for suntanning, relax-

Creative landscaping can enhance pool.

Pools can be designed for all swimming abilities.

ing or entertaining, this will be an important factor in the pool's design. If you want to add visual aesthetics, consider open-air structures such as gazebos, trellises, benches and screens shown as projects earlier in this book. These outdoor structures take up less room and appear "lighter" than cabanas and pool houses.

Where Will the Pool Be?

When planning where to put your pool, consider the location and angle of the sun and potential barriers between the sun and your pool. Some of the factors you'd be better off considering now than later are street noise, trees (especially whey they lose their leaves in Fall), privacy from your neighbors and security against unwanted guests as well as safety for invited guests.

What Kind of Swimming?

One of the first things to consider is how you will use the pool. Perhaps you want a place to relax and entertain, or maybe a backyard exercise center is your choice. If you have children, your pool could become a supervised playground for your future swimming and diving champions. You might even want to put in a spa or hot tub to complement your pool.

Each kind of pool has certain requirements. Defining the uses before you start to dig will help you choose the best design, location and size for your pool. Innovative products can increase your yard's possibilities.

Pools for Playing and Parties. If you're going to use your pool for splashing and playing in shallow water, or for parties and entertaining, your pool need only be a minimum of 3 ft. deep, with the average depth running between 4 and 5 feet.

Workouts and Warmups. If you're going to use your pool primarily for workouts, a lap pool may be perfect for your small yard space. A popular alternative for people who only want to use a pool for serious swimming, these long, narrow and shallow rectangular pools were once used only by competitive swimmers.

Lap pools usually range in width between 6 to 10 ft., are 3½ to 4 ft. deep and at least 30-ft. long. If there's a serious competitive swimmer in your family, you should plan to make the pool 25 meters long so that warmups and laps are done in the same conditions as these swimmers will find in competition.

Because these lap pools are long and thin, they can fit into small, narrow areas such as the back or side yard of a townhouse.

Exercising. A new, increasingly popular alternative if you're interested in exercising in a pool is the swim spa. These spas combine the benefits of soaking with those of lap swimming.

A powerful bank of water jets at one end of the spa generates a current to keep a swimmer in place. While stroking and kicking toward the water jets, the current pushes against the swimmer, making the swim continually "upstream." You can also put these spas indoors and use them for regular spa soaking.

Soaking and Relaxing. A hot item for all homes—condominiums, townhouses and single-family residences—is the portable spa. Portable spas can be set up inside or outdoors. They can be used on a patio or in a master bedroom or family room as the seasons change—as long as the floor can support the weight.

Brick decking gives an attractive addition to any pool.

Lap pools provide workout area for swimmers.

Swimming pools provide for any outdoor activity.

Lap pools in garden setting adds relaxation to workouts.

In-Ground Pools

An in-ground pool has many advantages in design and appearance and is a very durable structure if built and installed correctly.

Vinyl-liner Pools. The most popularly-priced type of in-ground pool, the vinyl-liner pool, is built with a flexible vinyl liner supported by a frame of aluminum, steel, plastic, masonry block or wood. In can be installed in a short period of time.

Vinyl-liner pools usually come in predefined sizes and shapes, although some manufacturers offer custom pools. Once the pool is constructed, most tears in the liner can be repaired without draining the pool. When properly maintained and when the water is kept balanced, the liner may last 10 to 15 years before it needs to be replaced with a new liner.

Gunite or Shotcrete Pools. If you want an unusual pool configuration, you might opt for a pool constructed of air-sprayed concrete. There are two construction processes commonly used—gunite and shotcrete. With both methods,

the concrete mixture of sand and cement is air-sprayed through the nozzle of a hose against a surface. Statistics show more than half the in-ground pools constructed each year are of concrete sprayed on steel reinforcing rods and finished with a fine coat of plaster. In-ground cement or gunite pool wall cracks are easily repaired with a small amount of plaster, caulking compound or epoxy putty once you lower the water below the damaged area.

Fiberglass Pools. Fiberglass pools are a third option for an in-ground pool. When installing a fiberglass pool, the excavation site is prepared in advance with rough plumbing before the single fiberglass shell is lowered into it. After the shell is adjusted, plumbing and electrical work are completed and the site is backfilled with sand.

Major advances in construction and installation of fiberglass pools have created hybrid pools that offer more flexibility than the single fiberglass shell. Hybrid units usually have fiberglass sidewalls with bottoms of concrete or vinyl.

Vinyl-lined pool.

Sprayed concrete pool.

One-piece fiberglass pool.

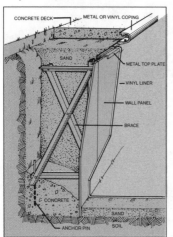

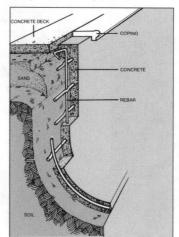

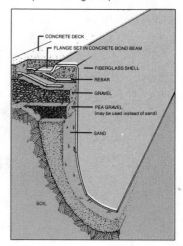

Aboveground Pools

If easy installation and moderate cost are your highest priorities when deciding what kind of pool to put in your yard, you may want to consider an aboveground pool. The aboveground pool is usually a good choice for the do-it-yourselfer.

An aboveground pool is usually round or oval, consisting of a structural shell and a vinyl liner. The pool's frame is usually aluminum or steel. Most of these pools can be set partially in the ground when it's necessary to put them in a sloping yard.

Many aboveground pools come in handy kits that can be assembled by two or three people. Using common household tools, you may be able to purchase a kit, assemble the swimming pool and enjoy a refreshing dip all within a week's time! But be sure your kit contains complete assembly and operating instructions before you take it home.

There's a brief primer on installing aboveground pools in Volume 23 of your *Popular Mechanics Do-it-Yourself Encyclopedia* that you'll want to review before you make a final decision about an aboveground pool.

Spas

Indoors, a portable spa can serve as the perfect focal point for a sun room, family room or exercise room. Outside, they fit well on a deck, patio or terrace. You can also use spas next to your swimming pool. Don't think you have to bring your portable spa indoors for the winter; an outdoor spa can be refreshing and healthy all year long, even in cold climates.

People have even adapted recycled casks from a winery for a hot tub or spa.

Spas can be put anywhere, even on deck by lake.

How Big? Spas come in many sizes to accommodate one, two, three or more people. If you're planning on doing lots of entertaining with family and friends, you should consider a larger spa. Larger spas are good for big families and for people over six-feet tall. If the spa is going to be your private little get-away-from-it-all space, then a smaller one will probably do.

How Much Water? The number of gallons of water your spa will hold will tell you two things: First, it will help you determine the overall weight of the unit and where you can put it. A gallon of water weighs about eight pounds. Second, it will give you an idea of how much water must be heated and an idea of how much energy will be needed to keep water warm.

Pool Essentials and Accessories

Most localities require that you install certain support equipment when building your pool. This support equipment circulates, filters and heats the water in your pool. It also helps to evenly distribute the chemicals you add to control purity and balance.

The Pump. The pump is the heart of your pool's support system. It circulates water through the filter and heater and then returns it to the pool. When choosing a pump, important factors to consider are its pumping capacity relative to the size of your pool, the operating costs and ease of maintenance.

The Filter. The filter's job is to keep your pool's water fresh and clean. There are three basic types of filters; the sand filter, diatomaceous earth and the cartridge filter. Each is designed to remove oils, grease and dirt from pool water.

Three common types of swimming pool filters.

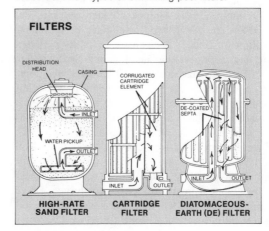

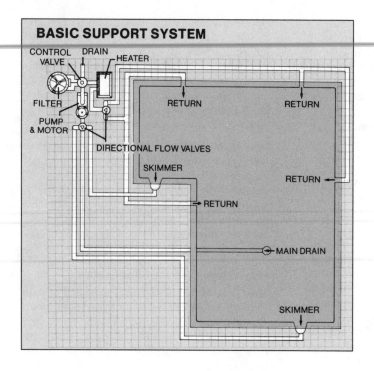

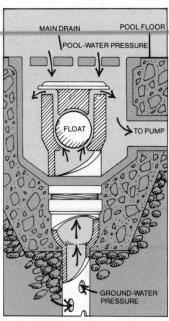

Hydrostatic valve *(above)* in main drain keeps underground water out of pool. Basic pool support system is shown at left.

The high-rate sand filter is the most popular type, partly because of its simplicity of operation and maintenance. Pool water is pumped through layers of sand inside a pressurized container. Dirt and grease particles are retained in the sand.

The obvious time to clean the filter is when the water is no longer clear. Don't wait until the pool water loses clarity, however, to check the filter. An increase in the pressure registered by a gauge on the filter tank or a reduction in water circulation are signs that the filter needs to be cleaned.

The high-rate sand filter is cleaned by backwashing. This is a process which reverses the flow of the water through the filter and pumps it out a waste line. Backwashing lifts the particles collected, raises the sand bed and cleans it.

The diacomaceous earth (D.E.) filter is another popular filter. The D.E. is a white powder that filters out even very small particles. There are various methods of cleaning D.E. filters, including backwashing. In most cases, the used D.E. material must be replaced whenever you clean the filter.

In a cartridge filter, pool water circulates through cartridges of fibrous material. These cartridges can be removed, hosed down and soaked in a cleaning agent. Cartridge filters are

relatively easy to clean and also have a low replacement cost. They should be replaced when they fail to maintain clear water in the pool.

The Heater. Most pool owners who have heaters agree that it is a vital factor in expanding their pool's use. Heaters can extend your swimming opportunities for more hours in the day and more months of the year, even year-round.

While the natural warmth of the sun does accomplish some pool heating, your supplemental heating options are gas, oil, electricity or solar. Some of these heat sources are more effective and less costly in different areas.

The Surface Skimmer. Skimmers draw in surface water accompanied by any floating dirt, leaves, oil or other debris while the pool drains remove objects suspended in the main body of water or those that fall to the bottom of the pool. Connected to the filtration system, skimmers help keep the water's surface clean and minimize the amount of debris that gets into the main body of the pool.

Most skimmers are built into the pool's filtration system, but there are portable skimmers that hang on the edge of the pool. These are especially useful for aboveground pools but can also be used for in-ground pools that did not have a skimming system when it was built.

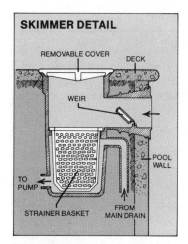

SKIMMER DETAIL

REMOVABLE COVER
DECK
WEIR
POOL WALL
TO PUMP
STRAINER BASKET
FROM MAIN DRAIN

Skimmer circulates and cleans water.

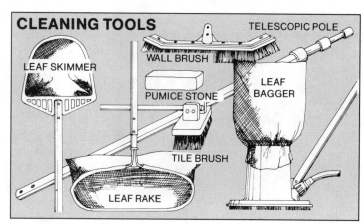

CLEANING TOOLS

TELESCOPIC POLE
LEAF SKIMMER
WALL BRUSH
PUMICE STONE
LEAF BAGGER
TILE BRUSH
LEAF RAKE

Basic pool cleaning tools you need on hand.

The Accessories. Automatic controls added to your pool system can turn the support system on and off, backwash to clean the filter and maintain the chlorine level.

Devices now on the market can measure mounting water pressure, a sign of a clogged or dirty filter, and activate valves to backwash the filtration system automatically. There are timers and dispensers to automatically feed chemicals into the water.

There are also various types of pool cleaners: vacuum systems for the floor of the pool, units that clean the surface and cleaning systems that use underwater hoses to direct objects toward the main drain.

Pool Landscaping

The location of your pool is very important. Building your pool where it will be in direct sunlight most of the day and where wind breaks will help retain heat will make it more enjoyable, and also will reduce your operating costs. Landscaping can create an environment that will enhance the natural beauty of your pool and home.

Trees, of course, are very effective windstoppers, but try to avoid locating the pool where falling or blowing leaves are a problem.

Building on Steep Hills. If your backyard has a steep slope, a hillside pool location is possible. In fact, a cliff-hanging pool perched high on a wooded hillside lends a gorgeous view as you swim. You should get professional advice on what type of support systems you'll need to ensure the pool is properly anchored. With proper decking of wood and brick, pool equipment and supports can be easily concealed.

Inside vs. Outside. If cold climates or other weather conditions shorten the time you use your pool, consider enclosing it partially or completely. An overhead cover or large air-circulated room are two options. Make it a dual purpose room—a swimming haven and greenhouse. Your pool can even start in your house and extend outdoors, possibly connected by a short underwater tunnel.

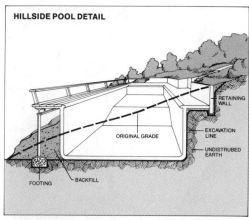

HILLSIDE POOL DETAIL

RETAINING WALL
ORIGINAL GRADE
EXCAVATION LINE
UNDISTURBED EARTH
FOOTING
BACKFILL

In-ground pools (above) or even aboveground pools (below) can be built into a hillside.

POOL
EXISTING GRADE
Pool must rest on firm, undisturbed soil.

Backyard Swimming Holes. You can change a plain backyard into a tropical paradise with the addition of a natural-shaped pool and some accessories and imagination: Wind rope around wooden piling lining a pierlike deck; dangle ivy over rocks; circulate water for a trickling waterfall. A pool that is painted or plastered a dark color will darken the water giving the effect of a lake or grotto. Be sure, however, that people can still see how deep the pool really is.

Multipurpose pool allows room for lap swimming with a shallow area for play and a deep end for diving.

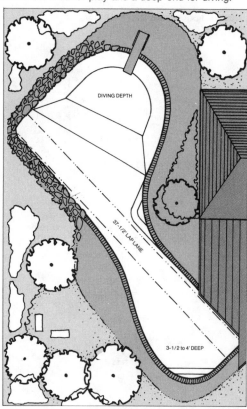

DIVING DEPTH

37-1/2' LAP LANE

3-1/2 to 4' DEEP

Have a Safe Swim

To get maximum enjoyment out of your pool, the National Spa and Pool Institute offers these tips to make your pool safe for you and your family:

- Never let anyone swim alone.

- If you aren't sure about someone's swimming ability, make sure they stay in shallow water and watch them closely.

- Establish "pool rules" that address the proper use of diving boards and slides, diving and non-diving areas, pool games, food and alcohol consumption, pool maintenance, use of electrical appliances and handling chemicals. Post these rules, in simple language, near the pool.

- Nobody should swim, dive or slide if they are under the influence of alcohol or drugs.

- Keep electrical appliances away from the pool. Use a ground fault circuit interrupter (GFCI) on any appliances that must be used poolside.

- If you use a pool cover, carefully read the manufacturer's directions for safe use. Always completely remove the cover before using your pool.

- Drain any standing water from the surface of your pool cover. Even a small amount of water may be enough for a small child to drown in.

Construction details for brick swimming pool deck.

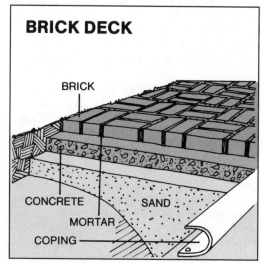

BRICK DECK

BRICK

CONCRETE   SAND

MORTAR

COPING

Pool Costs

Pools and spas are probably not as expensive as you think. According to a National Spa and Pool Institute survey in 1986, there are affordable packages available to fit every budget.

While prices will vary from place to place and special options like customized decks or landscaping may add additional costs, you can generally build or buy spas or pools within certain price ranges. For example, an aboveground pool generally costs between $1,400 and $3,000. An in-ground pool generally costs between $9,500 and $15,000 for a vinyl liner, between $12,500 and $18,000 for fiberglass, or between $13,000 and $28,000 for concrete.

Portable spas run between $2,000 and $3,500; custom-installed, engineered-plastic spas between $3,500 and $5,500 and concrete spas between $5,500 and $9,500. Hot tubs are usually between $3,400 and $5,000.

These prices are for a medium 15×30-ft. round or oval aboveground pool, a 15×30-ft. to 20×40-ft. in-ground pools and of the average-size spa or hot tub—all installed by a pool company. The more you can do yourself, the more you can reduce the final cost to you.

You'll also have annual operating costs to enjoy your pool. You'll need the chemicals to keep the water pure and clean. You may want to operate a heater to extend your swimming season in colder climates. And of course, there's the cost on your water bill to fill the pool.

While you just naturally assume that you'll fill a swimming pool with water, you don't immediately consider that cost as part of your pool planning. It will take about 39,000 gallons of water to fill a 20×40-ft. in-ground pool that's 3-ft. deep at the shallow end and 8-ft. at the deep end. That's enough water for you to soak in a hot bathtub every night for the next three years. When planning your pool accessories, the amount of water in your pool will dictate the size of heaters, filters and most of the other equipment in your support system. You can figure about 7½ gallons for each cubic foot of pool volume. In many parts of the country, you can buy pool water delivered in a tank truck at less cost than using water from a garden hose through your meter.

Keep Your Pool Looking New

A well-built and well-maintained pool will last for years. But after a while, even the best care will not prevent a pool from showing signs of age.

An old pool, or even a poorly maintained pool, is not a lost investment. A few repairs or simple refurbishing may be all that is needed. If major work is called for, you'll probably want a pool contractor to do it for you.

Repairing Cracks. In-ground cement or gunite pool walls may crack from earth movements under the shell or around the deck. Hairline cracks are easily repaired with a small amount of plaster, caulking compound or epoxy putty once you lower the water below the damaged area.

Check the extent of the crack. Large cracks may indicate a serious problem, possibly from soil movement or poor drainage. If a large crack should appear, it may be necessary to drain the pool, and you'll then want to consult a pool professional.

Replastering Concrete Pools. For best appearance, concrete pools should be replastered about every 10 to 15 years or repainted every 3 to 5 years. This is because daily contact with pool chemicals and changing water temperatures often cause flaking or chipping. Slight damage can be buffed and patched or painted over. In areas where mineral content or water hardness is excessive, it may be necessary to replaster sooner.

Mending a Vinyl Lining. You can repair most tears or punctures in a vinyl liner yourself. Some vinyl companies even offer underwater patching kits so you don't need to drain the pool for repairs. Tears longer than 2 to 3 inches are considered serious. If the repair is very costly to fix, it may be better to replace the liner.

Repairing Fiberglass Surfaces. Although fiberglass is strong and durable, in time the smooth finish may fade, chip or discolor. If this happens, check your warranty. Many manufacturers do cover surface deterioration. If the damage is small, patching the area may be all that is necessary. For larger areas, you may have to recoat the entire pool. A simple coat of epoxy paint may improve the appearance of an older fiberglass shell. Always follow the manufacturer's recommended procedures.

Tile Care. Tile trim along the inner edge of a pool can be very sensitive to shifts in the soil, and it can crack or pop off. Stronger adhesive can be used to put the tile back; but if there is actual structural damage, some excavation and rebuilding may be needed along the outer area of the pool.

Have a Safe Soak

To help you get the most enjoyment and relaxation from your spa, the National Spa and Pool Institute wants to encourage you to use it safely. Here are a few safety tips to follow:

- Never use the spa or hot tub when you're alone.

- Never use the spa or hot tub while or after drinking alcohol.

- Never use a spa or hot tub while or after using narcotics or medication that may cause sleepiness, drowsiness, or raise or lower blood pressure.

- Don't soak more than 15 minutes at one sitting in 104°F water. In lower temperatures (98° for example), most people can safely soak for slightly longer periods in one sitting. Be sure to check the water temperature before and while in the spa or hot tub.

- Be aware of the weakening effect of hot water and don't overdo exercises before or after your soak.

- For the sake of comfort and safety, people with long hair should tie their hair in a knot or bun to keep it out of the water and away from drains.

- People with heart disease, diabetes, high or low blood pressure or any serious illness, and pregnant women should not enter a spa or hot tub without first consulting with their doctor.

- Never allow children to use the spa or hot tub unsupervised.

- Explain to children using your spa or hot tub that they cannot *under any circumstances* dive or jump into it.

- A fence or natural barrier of sufficient height should be installed to limit access to the spa or hot tub. Lock doors or gates whenever soaking cannot be supervised.

- Don't place objects such as chairs or tables near the spa or hot tub fence that could allow a youngster to climb over and gain unsupervised access to your spa.

- Don't permit playful screaming for help (false alarms) that might mask a real emergency later.

Clean Spa Water. Chemistry of spa and hot tub water changes very quickly. These changes are caused by the high water temperatures, aeration of the water and the body chemistry of people using the spa or hot tub.

You should realize, for example that five people in a 500-700 gallon spa or tub equals about 250 people in an average size swimming pool in terms of perspiration and other compounds entering the water. Add to that the fact that high water temperature is ideal for algae and bacteria growth and you can understand why it is essential to maintain proper levels of disinfecting chemicals in the water.

Because these factors change water conditions rapidly, it is recommended that you check the water quality daily. To keep the spa or hot tub water fresh, use a water quality test kit. The kit is easy to use and will monitor the spa's chlorine/bromine (disinfectant) levels, the pH level, total alkalinity and calcium hardness.

When the water chemistry is not properly maintained, scaling, cloudiness, residue and bacteria growth can occur and this can be damaging to the support equipment and harmful to the health of those using the spa or hot tub.

Checklist for a Clean Pool. Keeping your pool clean can be easier by following a regular schedule. If you decide to do it yourself, a good checklist to follow for regular pool care is:

● Use a small hand-held leaf skimmer to help in cleaning the pool.

● Clean the tile and walls; tile is best cleaned with a soft brush and a pool tile cleaner. The cleaning of pool walls will depend on your surface: cement, vinyl or fiberglass. Follow the manufacturer's suggested procedures.

● Vacuum the pool at least once a week.

● Test the water frequently and add chemicals if necessary. Follow the manufacturer's directions.

● If the water turns cloudy, test for chemical balance. If necessary, backwash and service the filter.

● Keep the pool deck clean and clear of debris.

Additional information on maintaining the proper pH balance in your pool and annual service tips when you open and close your pool is part of the material about swimming pool maintenance in Volume 23 of your *Popular Mechanics Do-it-Yourself Encyclopedia.*

Paint the bottom of your pool a dark color to heighten the impression of greater depth.

Swimmers must be cautioned, however, about actual pool depth when diving or sliding into the water.

10 Garage Design and Construction

Garages come in all sizes and shapes. The selection of a garage is often determined by the limitations of the site and the size of the lot. Garages can add to the architectural lines of your house. They provide a protected place for your car during cold weather. Garages also provide protection against the weather for your family. You'll find these projects a useful addition to the other garage projects explained in Volume 11 of your *Encyclopedia*.

Carports are car-storage spaces, generally attached to the house, that have roofs and generally no sidewalls. To improve the appearance and utility of the carport, you can add storage cabinets on a side and at the end of the carport.

Garage Design Considerations

A critical design decision is the size of your garage. Cars now vary in size from small import models to large conversion vans and recreation vehicles. While the garage does not have to be designed to take all sizes of automobiles, it's best to provide a minimum interior depth of 21 feet. The inside width of a single garage should be 12 ft. or more. This makes the exterior size of a single garage approximately 14×22 feet. A double garage should be a minimum of 22×22 ft. (outside dimensions).

The foundation for an attached garage wall should extend below the frost line and about 8 in. above the finished-floor level. It should be no less than 6 in. thick, but it is usually more

Components of garage construction.

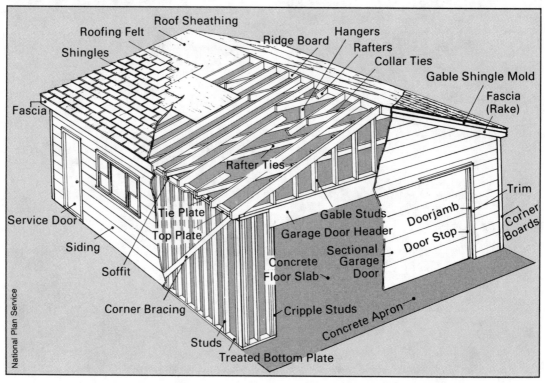

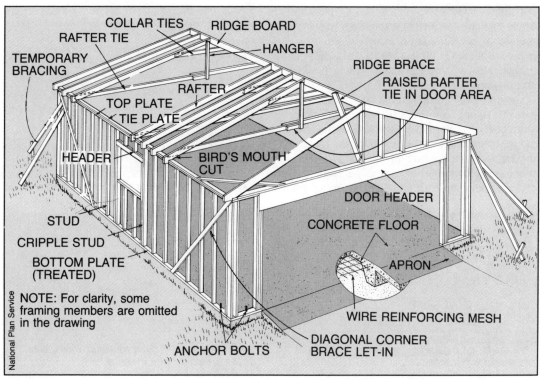

Typical construction details for any size garage.

because of the difficulty of trenching this width. Anchor the sill plate to the foundation wall with anchor bolts spaced about 8 ft. apart, at least two bolts in each sill piece. Extra anchors may be required at the sides of the main door. The framing of the sidewalls and the roof and the application of exterior wall material of an attached garage are similar to that of your home.

The interior finish of the garage is often a matter of choice. The studs may be left exposed or covered with some type of sheet material such as wallboard. Some building codes require that fire-resistant material be used on the wall between the house and an attached garage.

If fill is necessary below the floor, use well-compacted sand or gravel. If you use another type of soil fill, moisten it and let it settle before you pour the concrete. Unless you do, the floor will probably settle and crack.

Make the floor out of concrete at least 4 in. thick with a pitch of about 2 in. from the back to the front for drainage. Concrete reinforcement bar or wire is advisable, especially with wider or thicker slabs. The garage floor should be set about 1 in. above the drive or apron level and it should include an expansion joint.

Garage Doors

A sectional garage door is popular for both single and double bay garages. The sectional garage door has four or five horizontal hinged sections with tracks along sides and ceiling. You open it by lifting manually or using a motorized garage door opener. Doors for single-car garages are typically 9 ft. wide by 6½ or 7 ft. tall. Double-car garage doors are usually 16 by 6½ or 7 feet.

Garage doors vary in design, but most have panels with solid stiles and rails with panel fillers. Some include a glazed section for a window. Clearance above the top of the door for overhead doors should be about 12 inches. Low headroom brackets are available if such clearance is not possible.

Design the header beam over garage doors so the roof can withstand heavy snow loads. In wide openings, this may be a steel I-beam or a built-up wood beam. For spans of 8 or 9 ft., you can use two doubled 2×10s of structural grade wood in areas of low snow load. If the header will be supporting a second floor above it, use a steel I-beam or wide flange beam. Building codes in your area may be more specific about this.

Single-Car Garage

Many homeowners install a single-car garage to replace or supplement an older garage. These plans are for a 12×20 ft. (240 sq. ft.) single-car garage, but can you can modify them for any size or purpose.

Once you've determined the location for your garage, square off the site with chalk lines stretched between stakes installed outside the garage boundary. Dig the trench for the footing, making sure that the bottom is level. Then pour the footing concrete using ready-mixed concrete, a rented mixer or premixed concrete from

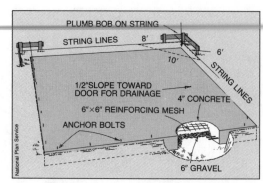

Laying out a garage floor for a concrete slab and footings.

Concrete for the garage floor is poured from truck and spread with a screed.

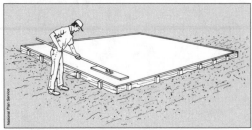

Smooth the surface of the concrete, making sure it slopes toward door for drainage.

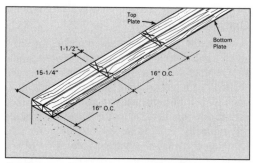

Simultaneously measure and mark both the top and bottom wall plates for accurate stud placement.

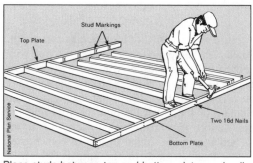

Place studs between top and bottom plates and nail into place from ends using two 16d nails.

a commercial supplier. Level the surface with a shovel and trowel. You can pour the concrete floor now or when you complete the garage. Make sure the floor slopes for correct drainage.

Check, again, the level of the footing before proceeding with the foundation. Then drop plumb lines from intersecting chalk lines to determine the exact corner point for the first blocks. Dampen the top of the footing, apply mortar and begin the first course of concrete or cinder blocks at the corner. Periodically check level as you go along.

After the last course, bolt or spike the sill plates to the foundation top. Backfill around the foundation after the concrete has cured.

Lay the sill plates out on the garage floor, mark them for stud location and place cut studs between them. Install the studs to the plates by nailing from top and bottom. Install doubled studs at door and window openings. Once you have constructed each wall as a unit, have someone help you lift it into position. Then check for plumb and anchor it with temporary 1×6 braces.

Check Building Codes

Garage plans shown in this chapter may not meet all requirements of local building codes for construction. Check with your local authorities or a structural architect before you start building any project shown in this chapter.

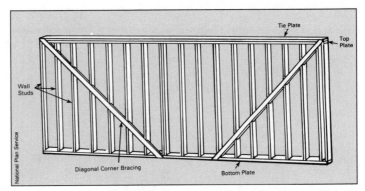

Diagonal corner bracing is installed once wall is completed and before it is lifted into place.

Completed wall is raised either by a crew or by using wall jacks.

Install sheathing plywood next and check for level and square. You can install sheathing horizontally or vertically depending upon patterns and size.

The roof is next. Lay out two lengths of 2×6 lumber and mark off measurements as shown in the plans. Cut all rafters and bevels at the same time to ensure consistency. Install the 2×6 ridge pole between end rafters using an extra pair of rafters at the center for support. Install the other rafters as shown.

Cover your single-car garage roof with exterior grade plywood sheathing. Then install roofing felt and shingles. Make sure the plywood is exterior grade so water does not damage the glue.

All that's left now is to install edge flashing, doors, windows and any trim. Your single-car garage is now complete.

Materials List
Single-Car Garage

Pcs	Size and description (use)
36	8×18″ cement blocks (foundation)
2	2×6×120″ lumber (ridge)
32	2×6×92″ lumber (rafters)
8	2×4×96″ lumber (plates)
7	2×4×96″ lumber (sills)
48	2×4×90″ lumber (studs)
12	48×96×½″ sheathing panels
9	48×96×½″ roof sheathing panels
2	36″ roofing felt rolls (15 lb.)
6	12×36″ 3-tab shingles
1	8×26×108″ lumber (door header)
1	84×96″ overhead garage door
	Cement
	Mortar

Fasteners:
8d, 16d galvanized nails
1¼″ galvanized roofing nails
8d finish nails
½×12″ anchor bolts, nuts, washers

Tools:
Portable circular or table saw, hammers, a level, measuring tape and cement tools

Check wall for plumb as it is braced in place.

Garage rafter cuts showing cuts at the wall and ridge.

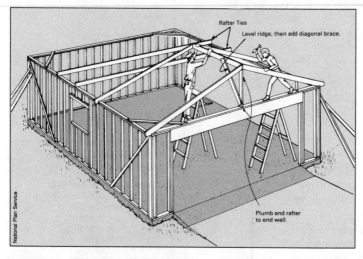

Rafters can be constructed in place, installing ridge between rafters.

Rafters can also be constructed on the garage floor, then installed.

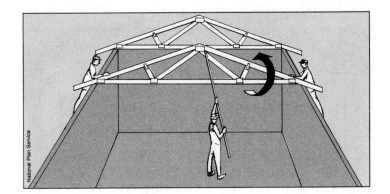

Rafter trusses are placed on top of the walls then swung into place.

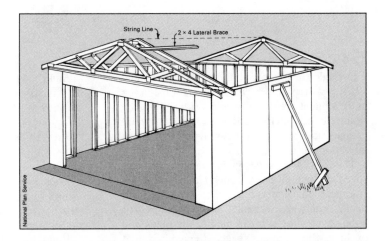

The trusses are then braced using a 2×4 lateral brace.

Roof sheathing, felt and shingles are then added.

Two-car garage with space for storage or a shop.

Two-Car Garage

The single-car garage, popular in the 1940s and 1950s, was replaced by the double garage in the more affluent 1960s, 1970s and 1980s. While the small car has encouraged 1½-car (18-ft. wide) garages, it is still the two-car garage that is the most popular today.

This 24×24-ft. double garage includes storage space that can save you from building a separate storage shed. You can use the storage area to install shelving, cabinets, workbenches, or hobby tables, or you can modify the plans and exclude the storage space. Remember that changing rafter design requires the help of a structural architect.

The first step in constructing your double garage is to pour the foundation. You can either do it yourself or a contractor can install it for you. You'll need approximately 18 cubic yards of readymix concrete: 3 for the footing, 8 for the foundation walls and another 7 for the floor itself. Remember to use ½-in. rebar and a wire mesh for reinforcement.

As the concrete dries, set the anchor bolts 1¾ in. from the edge with at least 2½ in. of the bolt above the surface.

Once dried, install the 2×4 bottom plate flush to the outside of the foundation. You'll have to mark and drill ¾-in. holes for the anchor bolts to slip up through the plate. Don't install the plate yet.

Build each wall horizontally on the concrete slab and lift it into place. Lay the predrilled 2×4 bottom plate and one 2×4 top plate side by side. Mark the position of each stud 16-in. o.c. Insert the studs between the plates and nail through the plates into the ends of the studs using two 16d nails at each connection.

Make sure the first wall is square, then lay the 1×4 in. corner brace diagonally across the top, as shown. Mark its location across each stud. Use your circular saw to cut ¾-in.-deep grooves in the studs to make room for the bracing. Knock out the grooved wood with a chisel. Install the brace with two 8d nails at each stud.

Then, with help, erect each wall as shown and secure in place with a temporary brace. Make sure the walls are aligned so that the holes in the bottom plate accommodate the anchor bolts.

Build the other three walls the same way, making sure you install doors and windows at the correct location and with a sufficient header. Install 2×4 tie plates between walls with 16d nails. Refer to the plans.

Next, cut the garage door header to length and assemble it with 16d nails. Install 2×4 cripple studs at each side of the door opening. Lift the header into position, set it on the cripples and nail into place.

Install rafter ties 48-in. o.c. across the top plates and tack them in place. Cut and install the end rafters. Then install the ridge board. Now you can install the remaining rafters under the ridge board and between the end rafters. Nail collar ties to the rafters.

Make sure that you allow proper clearance for installation of the garage door and garage door opener if you're going to put one in. Garage door openers typically require a wood mounting plate built under or between the rafters on which the mechanism is mounted. There should be an electrical outlet within 12 in. of the opener.

Make sure the rafters are level at the center of the span. Then add 1×4-in. hangers between the rafters and ties. Install 2×4 gable studs and

Materials List
Two-Car Garage

Key	Pcs	Size and description (use)
A	2	2×12×216″ lumber (garage door header)
B	26	2×8×168″ lumber (rafters)
C	2	2×6×192″ lumber (garage door framing)
D	5	2×6×168″ lumber (rafter ties)
E	5	2×6×120″ lumber (rafter ties)
F	1	2×4×192″ lumber (plates)
G	1	2×4×192″ lumber (garage door blocking)
H	2	2×4×168″ lumber (plates)
J	12	2×4×144″ lumber (plates)
K	12	2×4×120″ lumber (gable studs)
L	72	2×4×96″ lumber (studs)
M	2	2×4×96″ lumber (door header)
N	6	2×4×96″ lumber (cripple studs)
P	12	1×8×168″ lumber (soffit)
Q	1	1×8×120″ lumber (gable end drop)
R	4	1×6×168″ lumber (fascia)
S	11	1×6×120″ lumber (collar ties)
T	2	1×6×120″ lumber (rafter splice plate)
U	2	1×6×120″ lumber (ridge board)
V	6	1×4×144″ lumber (corner braces)
W	3	1×4×120″ lumber (hangers)
	6	1×4×96″ door jambs
	24	48×96×⅝″ plywood siding
	23	48×96×½″ CD exterior plywood
	2	36″ 15 lb. roofing felt
	8	Squares 235 lb. asphalt shingles
	1	16×7′ garage door track/hardware
	1	32×80×¾″ service door with hardware
	2	22×31×½″ window units
	6	96″ door stop
	5	120″ Z-flashing
	1	Door lockset

Fasteners:

8d, 16d galvanized nails
1¼″ galvanized roofing nails
8d finish nails
½× 12″ anchor bolts, nuts, washers

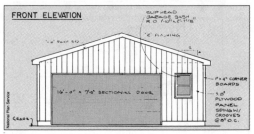

FRONT ELEVATION

Finishing detail for front of double garage.

blocking as shown. You have now framed your garage.

Beginning at the eave, install ½-in. exterior plywood sheathing over the roof rafters. Stagger the joints. Apply roofing felt, then shingles ¾ in. beyond the trim board face.

Install door casings, using wood shims to adjust to the correct width.

Install insulation or vapor barrier on the outside of studs, then put up siding with 8d siding nails 12-in. o.c.

Nail trim on the eaves and corners. Install the service door, windows and garage door following the manufacturer's instructions.

Finally, paint or stain the siding and trim. Do a final inspection of your new two-car garage. Then start filling it up.

Construction detail for front of two-car garage.

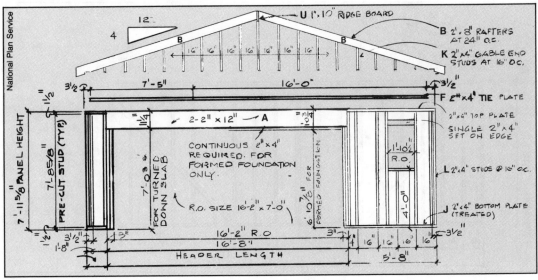

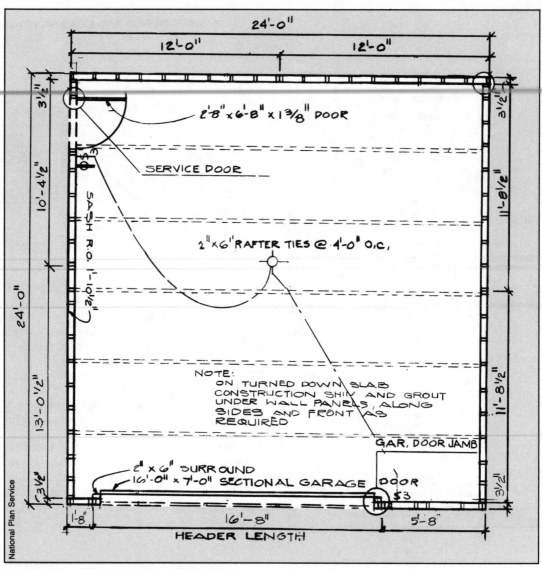

Plan view for a two-car garage *(above)*. Construction
details *(below)* for the back wall of this garage.

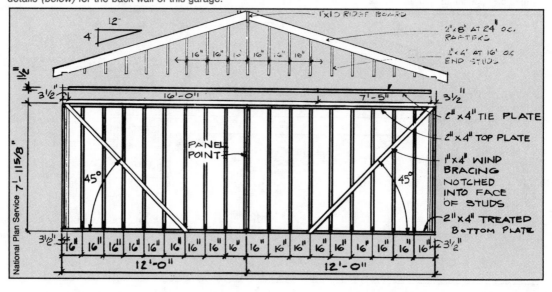

Check Building Codes

These plans for a three-car garage may not meet all requirements of local building codes for construction. Check with your local authorities or a structural architect before you start building this project.

Three-Car Garage

The three-car garage was, until recently, a luxury only for the rich. Today's family may have three or more drivers and as many cars. Also, some homeowners are constructing three-car garages with the third bay for a boat, camper, snowmobiles or other recreation vehicles. The third bay could also serve as a full workshop, office or storage area, making the three-car garage a practical outdoor structure for many families.

This plan guides you in constructing a 22×32-ft. triple garage with one single and one double door. There are also two windows and a service door. You can easily modify this design to add service doors, windows or even build a four-car garage.

Before you begin, read over this section until you are completely familiar with the steps and requirements. Even if you have a contractor build your garage, you'll be a wise consumer if you understand the procedures.

The foundation requires approximately 21 cubic yards of concrete: 4 for the footing, 9 for the foundation walls and another 8 for the floor itself. Reinforce the foundation with ½-in. rebar and a wire mesh. Set the anchor bolts 1¾ in. from the edge with at least 2½ in. of the bolt above the surface.

After the foundation and floor have completely cured and backfilled, lay the 2×4 bottom plate around the perimeter of the foundation. Then mark and drill ¾-in. holes for the anchor bolts to slip up through the plate.

Build the walls for your three-car garage on the concrete slab and lift them into place. To do this, first lay the predrilled 2×4 bottom plate and one 2×4 top plate side by side on their edges. Mark the position of each stud with an "X" 16-in. o.c. Then place the studs between the plates and nail through them into the ends of the studs with two 16d nails at each connection.

You now need to verify that this first wall is square. Then, lay the 1×4 corner brace diagonally across the top, as shown, and mark its location across each stud. Then cut ¾-in.-deep grooves in the studs for the bracing. Remove excess wood with a chisel. Lay the brace in place and nail at each stud with two 8d nails.

It's time to raise the first wall into place. You'll need some helpers or you can rent wall jacks. Wall jacks are mounted on 2×4s slipped under the top plate and jacked to lift the wall. Place blocks at the bottom plate so that the wall doesn't slip as it goes up. Make sure you move from jack to jack to ensure that the wall goes up evenly. Then secure the wall in place with a temporary brace.

Construct the other walls in the same manner. Put in headers for the the garage door, service door and window as you build the walls. Brace headers with 2×4 cripple studs at each side of the opening. Put up each wall as you make it. Then attach 2×4 tie plates with 16d nails between the walls and remove temporary bracing.

Check your wall again for trueness. Measure diagonally from corner to corner to make sure each wall is square.

To construct the roof, first install rafter ties 48-in. o.c. across the top plates and tack them in position. Then cut and install the end rafters as shown.

Install the ridge board next. Continue by installing the remaining rafters under the ridge board and between the end rafters. Fasten collar ties to the rafters. Then install 1×4 hangers between the rafters and ties, and also between the 2×4 gable studs and blocking.

Now use ½-in. CD exterior plywood sheathing over the roof rafters beginning at the eaves. Make sure you stagger the joints for strength. To finish the roof, overlap roofing felt as you roll it horizontally across the sheathing.

Then install 3-tab asphalt shingles beginning ¾ in. beyond the trim board face, staggering the tabs to minimize seepage.

To finish off your three-car garage, install the garage and service door casings. Place insulation material on the outside of the wall framing and nail siding with 10½ in. exposure using 8d nails. Then nail trim on the eaves and corners. Paint or stain the siding and trim. Finally, install garage doors following manufacturer's instructions and the directions below.

Garage door uses special hardware and hanging techniques.

Installing Overhead Garage Doors

While garage doors were constructed for many years much like a double door, most today are "overhead" doors; that is, they swing up and out of the way. The majority of today's overhead doors are sectional; they break into horizontal sections mounted on a track extending along the sides and under the ceiling frame. Here you'll see how to install single and double sectional overhead garage doors.

Measure the door opening height and width. Most require at least 12 in. clearance above the door for the rail and apparatus, though brackets are available for lower or higher clearance. You need a minimum of 3 in. of side room. At the same time, verify that the door opening is square. If not, shim or replace side and head jambs to bring them into square.

Stack the door sections in the opening from bottom to top. Use thin lumber scraps to shim the bottom so it is level and true. Then assemble and mount the vertical track to the front wall at each side of the opening. Fasten the track brackets to the wall.

Next, install the horizontal track to the ceiling, using the method suggested by the manufacturer. Make sure the track and ceiling are level and square to the door opening and to each other. Then, tighten all brackets and fasteners. Install the tension springs, but wait until you paint and glaze the door before making final adjustments.

Overhead garage door maintenance is simple: inspect cables, rollers, springs, brackets and pulleys twice a year and lubricate once a year.

Materials List
Three-Car Garage

Pcs	Size and description (use)
2	2×12×216″ lumber (garage door header)
2	2×12×120″ lumber (garage door header)
2	2×6×192″ lumber (garage door framing)
50	2×6×168″ lumber (rafters)
2	2×6×168″ lumber (sash blocking)
7	2×6×144″ lumber (rafter ties)
3	2×6×144″ lumber (gable blocking)
7	2×6×120″ lumber (rafter ties)
7	2×4×192″ lumber (wall plate)
2	2×4×192″ lumber (garage door blocking)
1	2×4×192″ lumber (garage door framing)
6	2×4×168″ lumber (wall plate)
4	2×4×144″ lumber (gable nailer)
1	2×4×120″ lumber (garage door framing)
2	2×4×120″ lumber (garage door blocking)
78	2×4×96″ lumber (studs)
15	2×4×96″ lumber (cripples)
10	2×4×96″ lumber (wall plate)
9	2×4×96″ lumber (gable studs)
8	2×2×96″ lumber (soffit nailer)
1	1×12×144″ gable end drop
2	1×8×216″ lumber (ridge board)
4	1×8×168″ lumber (fascia and soffit)
6	1×8×144″ lumber (fascia and soffit)
2	1×6×168″ lumber (rafter tie plate)
11	1×6×120″ lumber (collar ties)
6	1×4×144″ lumber (corner brace)
4	1×4×96″ lumber (hangers)
4	1×4×96″ corner board
4	1×3×96″ corner board
909	sf 7⁄16×12″ horizontal siding
30	48×96×½″ CD exterior plywood
	58′ single mold gable
3	36″ 15 lb. roofing felt
10	Squares 235 lb. asphalt shingles
1	16×7′ garage door/track/hardware
1	9×7′ garage door/track/hardware
1	32×80×¾″ service door with hardware
2	64×27″ window units

Fasteners:
8d, 10d, 16d galvanized nails
7⁄8″ galvanized roofing nails
8d finish nails
½×12″ anchor bolts, nuts, washers

SHINGLED RIDGE

235# SELF-SEAL ASPHALT SHINGLES

1" x 8" FASCIA

1" x 4" & 1" x 3" CORNER BOARDS

16'-0" x 7'-0" UP AND OVER DOOR

9'-0" x 7'-0" UP & OVER DOOR

FRONT ELEVATION

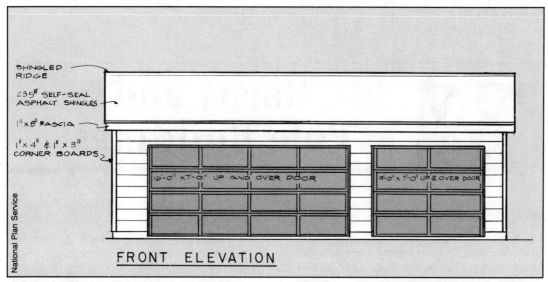

Finishing detail for front of three-car garage *(above)*.

Construction details *(below)* for sides of garage.

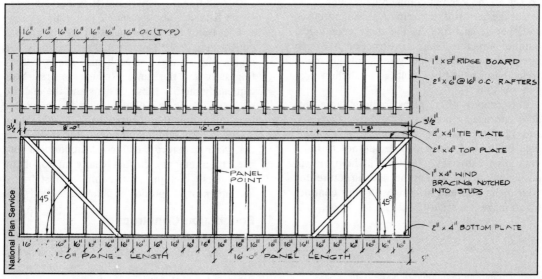

16" 16" 16" 16" 16" 16" O.C (TYP)

1" x 8" RIDGE BOARD

2" x 6" @ 16" O.C. RAFTERS

3½"

8'-0"   16'-0"   7'-5"

2" x 4" TIE PLATE

2" x 4" TOP PLATE

PANEL POINT

1" x 4" WIND BRACING NOTCHED INTO STUDS

45°   45°

2" x 4" BOTTOM PLATE

16" 16" 16" 16" 16" 16" 16" 16" 16" 16" 16" 16" 16" 16" 16" 16" 16" 16" 16" 16"

1'-0" PANEL LENGTH   16'-0" PANEL LENGTH   5"

Construction details *(below)* for back of garage.

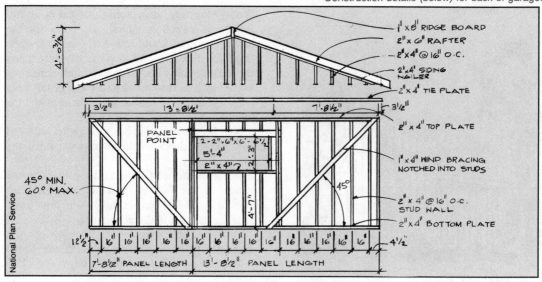

4'-0 3/8"

1" x 8" RIDGE BOARD

2" x 6" RAFTER

2" x 4" @ 16" O.C.

2" x 4" SIDING NAILER

2" x 4" TIE PLATE

3½"   13'-8½"   7'-8½"   3½"

2" x 4" TOP PLATE

PANEL POINT

2 - 2" x 6" x 6' - 6½"

5'-4"

2" x 4"

2'-3"

1" x 4" WIND BRACING NOTCHED INTO STUDS

45° MIN. 60° MAX.

4'-7"

45°

2" x 4" @ 16" O.C. STUD WALL

2" x 4" BOTTOM PLATE

12½" 16" 16" 16" 16" 16" 16" 16" 16" 16" 16" 16" 16" 16"   4½"

7'-8½" PANEL LENGTH   13'-8½" PANEL LENGTH

Barns and Pole Buildings

The barn of yesterday was not only a shelter for family livestock, but also a place where children loved to play. Today, the homestead barn is nearly extinct as farms become subdivisions and horses are boarded at commercial stables.

Yet the barn still serves many useful purposes and, per square foot, is the most economical outdoor structure. Barn construction has seen many changes over the years and, in many areas, barns have been replaced by the low-cost pole building.

This chapter offers plans for four large outdoor storage structures: 12×12-ft., 12×16-ft. and 12×20-ft. gambrel barns, and a 28×40-ft. pole building. Even if you decide not to build your own barn, this chapter will help you in designing the most appropriate structure for your own needs and working with your contractor to make it a reality.

Barn with familiar gambrel roof shape. This basic shape is typical of the three different size barns shown in this chapter.

The Gambrel Barn

For much of its Western history, the barn has typically been constructed with a gambrel roof. This type of roof is both low cost and efficient. It allows a higher ceiling and more loft space than with traditional pitch roofs. It is easy to construct from readily obtainable materials.

The following three gambrel barns are all constructed in the same manner. Since only the dimensions change for each size, the construction steps are the same. Read them first. You can easily modify these designs and the materials lists to come up with your own design: wider, longer, shorter, taller. First check local building codes to get a building permit and to make sure that your structure meets construction and setback requirements. In fact, many metropolitan areas have building restrictions against barns and other large outdoor structures.

Foundation Construction

Your foundation can either be wood or concrete. The floor can be dirt, wood or concrete, depending on how you will use it, local weather conditions and your budget.

Wood Flooring If installing a wood floor, follow these directions: First, dig holes for the piers. The piers should be 3 to 6 in. below the frost line depending on severity of winters and the local building codes. Install reinforcing rods in the block piers and make sure you install strap anchors before the mortar sets. Then backfill the foundation.

Nail the 2×8-in. side beams together with 16d nails. Place them on the piers and attach the strap anchors.

Install metal joist hangers 16-in. o.c. on the inside of the beams, making sure they are aligned parallel. Then set the 2×8-in. floor joists into the hangers and nail in place.

Once you have installed the floor joists, begin laying the plywood flooring perpendicular to the joists. Use 8d nails 6 in. apart at edges and 12 in. apart on other joists.

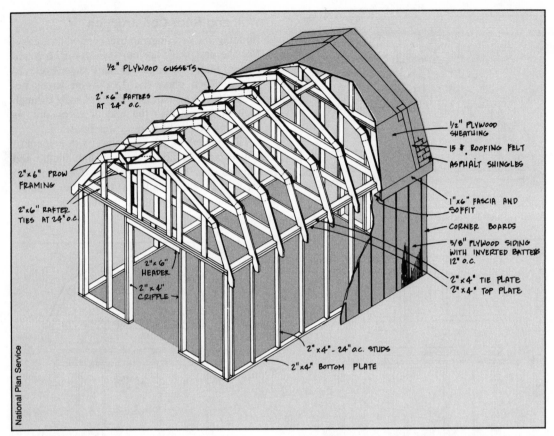

½" PLYWOOD GUSSETS

2"×6" RAFTERS
AT 24" O.C.

½" PLYWOOD
SHEATHING

15 # ROOFING FELT

ASPHALT SHINGLES

2"×6" PROW
FRAMING

2"×6" RAFTER
TIES AT 24" O.C.

1"×6" FASCIA AND
SOFFIT

CORNER BOARDS

5/8" PLYWOOD SIDING
WITH INVERTED BATTENS
12" O.C.

2"×6"
HEADER

2"×4"
CRIPPLE →

2"×4" TIE PLATE
2"×4" TOP PLATE

2"×4"-24"o.c. STUDS

2"×4" BOTTOM PLATE

National Plan Service

Construction details for any of the three gambrel barns shown in this chapter.

While size of the three barns may differ, the basic construction techniques are the same.

Concrete Slab Floor If you are installing a concrete slab, first stake out the slab area as shown in the plans. Make sure the corners are square, then dig the foundation trench around the perimeter 12 in. deep, 8 in. wide at the bottom and 16 in. wide at the top, as shown.

Next, lay out forms for the floor slab using 2-in. lumber. Make sure the top edges of the forms are at the desired floor height and completely level. Brace them securely. Spread gravel fill evenly to within 4 in. of the top of the form.

Check the materials list to see how much concrete you'll need for your slab floor. Most do-it-yourselfers order concrete through a firm that delivers it to the site. Try to have it delivered on a morning where temperatures aren't

below freezing and afternoon temperatures aren't expected to be above 85°, if possible. If necessary, you can protect your new concrete with moist burlap. You want it to dry out or cure slowly without freezing or baking. Be sure your site is ready for the concrete when it's delivered.

Once your concrete is poured, begin spreading and leveling it. You can rent or borrow concrete working tools. Make sure you install the anchor bolts into the concrete before it sets. Place them 1¾ in. from each edge and 2½ to 3 in. above the surface.

After the concrete has set, lay the 2×4 bottom plates in place and on top of the bolts. Strike the plates with a hammer to mark the locations of the anchor bolts. Then drill out ¾-in. holes at each mark. Install the plates.

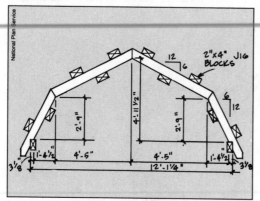

Rafter jig plan for 12′×20′ barn.

Wall and Roof Construction

Building and erecting gambrel barn walls is easy. For the first wall, lay out the 2×4-in. top and bottom plates on edge and mark them every 24 inches. Then place the 2×4×84-in. studs between them and hammer two 16d nails through each plate and into the end of each stud, as shown in other chapters of this book.

Tilt the wall panels into place with helpers or a wall jack. Make sure the wall is plumb and square, then brace it in place. Construct and erect the other walls in the same manner, fastening them together at corners.

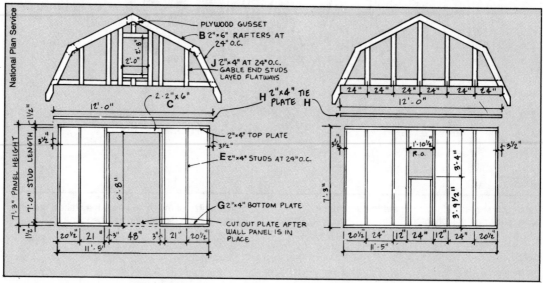

Construction details (above) for front and back.

Finishing details (below) for front and back of barn.

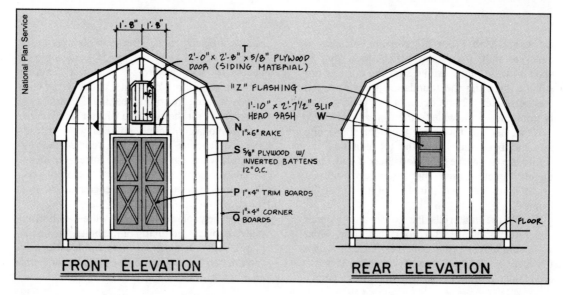

Construct roof trusses in an assembly-line fashion by laying out the first truss on a board or plywood covered floor. Then nail blocks on each side of the members with duplex form nails. Install the first truss, making sure it is correct, before building the others. Set them aside as they are built for later installation.

One at a time, lift and install the roof trusses. The easiest way is to lay the truss base atop the side walls with the ridge pointing down, then attach a rope to the top of the ridge and hoist it up into position. Once in place, nail the truss to the top plate and brace laterally. Frame in the gable ends as shown in the plans.

Install the 2×6 soffit nailing blocks. Install plywood roof sheathing with 8d nails. Roll the roofing felt into place, install the metal drip edges and apply asphalt shingles.

Next, install corner boards and frieze boards. Nail the 1×6-in. soffit, fascia and rake boards into place. Then install the window unit and nail siding to the walls. Construct the door with a frame, siding, trim boards and hardware, as shown. Paint or stain siding and trim.

Check Building Codes

These gambrel barn plans may not meet all requirements of local building codes for construction. Check with your local authorities or a structural architect before you start building any of these barn projects.

Materials List
12×12-ft. Gambrel Barn
WALLS AND ROOF

Key	Pcs	Size and description (use)
A	7	2×6×144″ lumber (rafter ties)
B	14	2×6×120″ lumber (rafters, trim)
C	1	2×6×120″ lumber (door header, trim)
D	1	2×6×120″ lumber (roof prow)
E	18	2×4×168″ lumber (wall studs, trim)
F	1	2×4×168″ lumber (soffit blocks)
G	4	2×4×144″ lumber (bottom plate)
H	9	2×4×144″ lumber (plates, braces)
J	6	2×4×120″ lumber (gable studs)
K	1	1×10×96″ lumber (false beam casing)
L	2	1×6×168″ lumber (eave fascia)
M	2	1×6×168″ lumber (soffit)
N	4	1×6×144″ lumber (rake fascia)
P	1	1×4″×116′ lumber (door trim, casing)
Q	6	1×4×168″ lumber (corner, frieze boards)
R	1	1×4×96″ lumber (false beam soffit)
S	15	48×96×5/8″ plywood (siding)
T	1	48×96×5/8″ plywood (doors)
U	8	48×96×1/2″ plywood (roof sheathing)
V	2	48×96×1/2″ plywood (gussets)
W	1	22×31½″ window sash unit
X		70′ metal drip edge
Y		3⅓ squares 235 lb. asphalt shingles
Z		20′ molding (door stop)

WOOD FLOOR

Pcs	Size and description (use)
36	8×8×16″ concrete blocks (piers)
10	2×8×144″ lumber (floor joists)
4	2×8×144″ lumber (box sill beam)
5	48×96×3/4″ plywood (floor)

CONCRETE FLOOR

Pcs	Size and description (use)
	2 cubic yards gravel (base)
	4 cubic yards concrete
	144 sq. ft. wire mesh (reinforcement)
13	10×½″ anchor bolts, washers, nuts

Construction and finishing details for sides of barns.

Side dimensions will differ with each size barn.

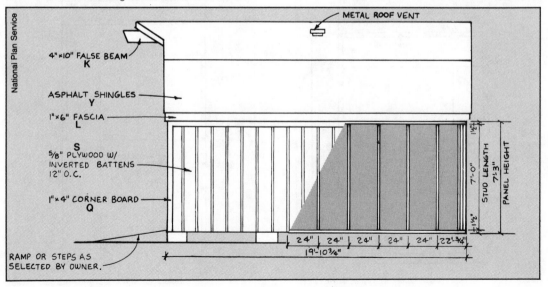

National Plan Service

METAL ROOF VENT

4″×10″ FALSE BEAM
K

ASPHALT SHINGLES
Y

1″×6″ FASCIA
L

S
5/8″ PLYWOOD W/ INVERTED BATTENS 12″ O.C.

1″×4″ CORNER BOARD
Q

RAMP OR STEPS AS SELECTED BY OWNER.

7′-0″ STUD LENGTH
7′-3″ PANEL HEIGHT

24″ 24″ 24″ 24″ 24″ 22′-3/4″
19′-10¾″

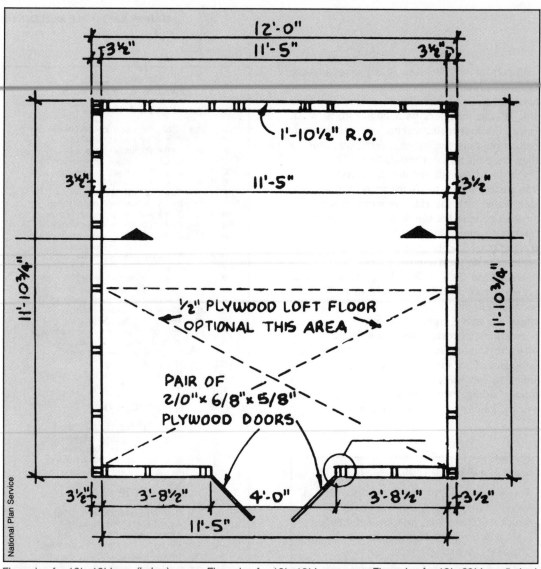

12'-0"
11'-5"
3½"　　　　　　　　　　　　3½"

1'-10½" R.O.

11'-5"

3½"　　　　　　　　　　　　3½"

11'-10¾"　　　　　　　　　　11'-10¾"

½" PLYWOOD LOFT FLOOR
OPTIONAL THIS AREA

PAIR OF
2/0"× 6/8"× 5/8"
PLYWOOD DOORS

3½"　3'-8½"　　4'-0"　　3'-8½"　3½"

11'-5"

National Plan Service

Floor plan for 12′×16′ barn *(below)*.　Floor plan for 12′×12′ barn *(above)*　Floor plan for 12′×20′ barn *(below)*.

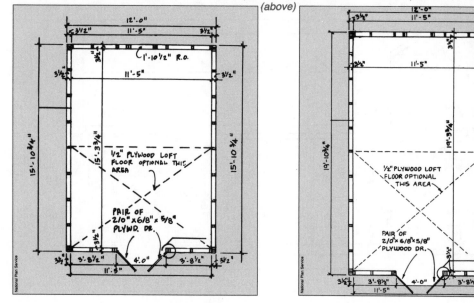

12'-0"
11'-5"
3½"　　　3½"
3½"
1'-10½" R.O.
11'-5"
3½"

15'-10¾"　15'-3¾"　15'-10¾"

½" PLYWOOD LOFT
FLOOR OPTIONAL THIS
AREA

PAIR OF
2/0"×6/8"× 5/8"
PLYWD. DR.

3½"　3'-8½"　4'-0"　3'-8½"　3½"
11'-5"

National Plan Service

12'-0"
11'-5"
3½"　　　3½"

11'-5"

19'-10¾"　19'-3¾"　19'-10¾"

½" PLYWOOD LOFT
FLOOR OPTIONAL
THIS AREA

PAIR OF
2/0"× 6/8"× 5/8"
PLYWOOD DR.

3½"
3½"　3'-8½"　4'-0"　3'-8½"　3½"
11'-5"

National Plan Service

Pole Building

The pole building is one of the most cost-effective storage buildings. You can use it for automobiles, machinery, livestock, recreation vehicles, storage, businesses or any combination of these.

The plan is for a 28×40 pole building with a 14-ft. ceiling, two overhead doors and one large sliding door. Of course, you can modify this plan for various uses. Make sure that an architect checks any changes to the plan, especially those that affect the roof trusses, before you begin construction. Lumber touching the earth should be pressure-treated to minimize insect and moisture damage.

First make sure that you meet all local codes and regulations and that you understand the requirements of your building permit. Stake out the perimeter of your pole building. Stretch your

Pole building is an inexpensive structure for the space it provides.

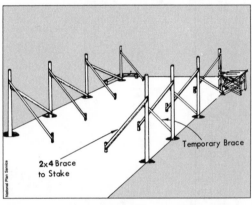

Poles are set, then staked with temporary bracing to ensure they remain plumb.

string line so that it marks the perimeter of the proposed walls. Then remove and compact dirt as required. If you are installing a concrete floor, do so now.

Mark the locations of poles with stakes, then dig pole holes 48 to 60 in. deep and 30 in. or more wide using a power auger or backhoe. Clean the holes of water and loose materials before installing concrete footings.

The best four poles become your corners. Install them in the holes and set them square 1½ in. inside the string line. Tamp earth into the bottom third of the holes. Set the corner poles with temporary 2×4 diagonal braces as shown, making sure the braces don't interfere with the girders when they are installed later. The braces will later become the girts. Duplex-head nails will securely anchor the braces while allowing easy removal.

Once you have installed the four corner poles, you can place the intermediate poles using 2×4 diagonal braces and ground stakes. Make sure you place all poles according to the plan.

Install girders by first marking ground level at the bottom of each pole with a partly driven nail. Then measure up each pole 158¾ in. and drive another marking nail. This is the bottom height of the 2×12 girders. Nail 2×6 girder support blocks on the inside and outside of each pole using 40d nails as shown. Prepare and install girders to butt the center line of each pole.

Poles are set into a concrete footing with gravel or tamped earth fill, then plumbed and staked.

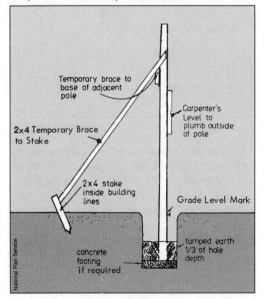

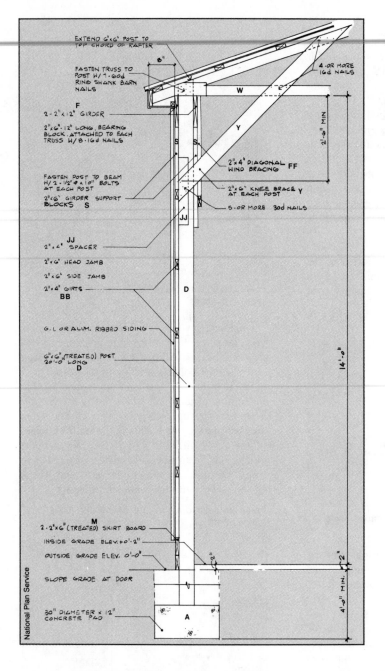

EXTEND 6"×6" POST TO
TOP CHORD OF RAFTER

FASTEN TRUSS TO
POST W/ 7-60d
RING SHANK BARN
NAILS

4-OR MORE
16d NAILS

F

2-2"×12" GIRDER

2"×6"-12" LONG, BEARING
BLOCK ATTACHED TO EACH
TRUSS W/ 8-16d NAILS

W

Y

2'-0" MIN.

2"×4' DIAGONAL
WIND BRACING   FF

FASTEN POST TO BEAM
W/ 2-1/2"Ø×10" BOLTS
AT EACH POST

2"×6" GIRDER SUPPORT
BLOCKS S

2"×6" KNEE BRACE Y
AT EACH POST

5-OR MORE 30d NAILS

JJ

JJ
2"×4' SPACER

2"×6" HEAD JAMB

2"×6" SIDE JAMB

2"×4" GIRTS
BB

D

G.I. OR ALUM. RIBBED SIDING

6"×6" (TREATED) POST
20'-0" LONG
D

14'-0"

M
2-2"×6" (TREATED) SKIRT BOARD

INSIDE GRADE ELEV. +0'-2"

OUTSIDE GRADE ELEV. 0'-0"

SLOPE GRADE AT DOOR

4'-0" MIN.   2"

30" DIAMETER × 12"
CONCRETE PAD

A

National Plan Service

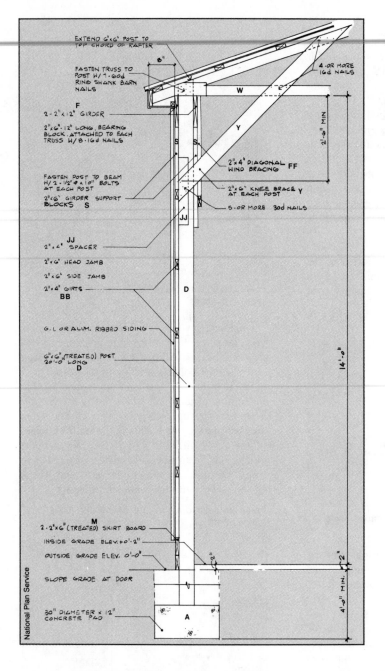

Pole building footing, wall and cap
construction details.

Install the 2×6×18-in. truss tie-down blocks
between doubled girders as shown. Then check
and realign poles and girders to make sure they
are true and level. Finish girder nailing and
install diagonal wind bracing. Finally, fill and
tamp all holes, crowning the tops for water
runoff.

You'll need a crane or hoist lift to install
trusses constructed on the ground as single
units. Beginning at one end of the pole building,
install and then brace each truss laterally to
ensure that it remains true. Install 2×4 spacer
blocks and knee bracing as shown.

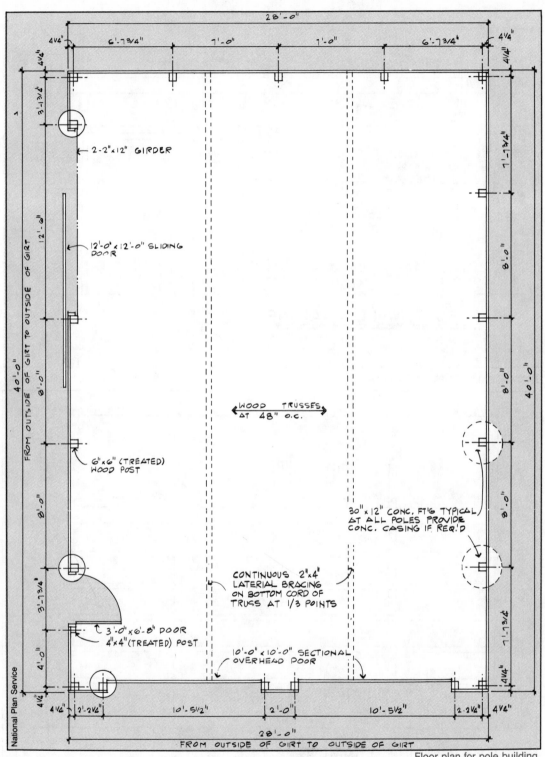

Floor plan for pole building.

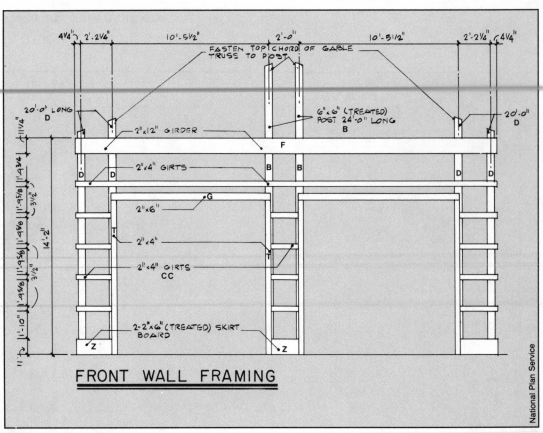

FRONT WALL FRAMING

Labels visible in figure:
FASTEN TOP CHORD OF GABLE TRUSS TO POST
6"×6" (TREATED) POST 24'-0" LONG
B
20'-0" LONG
D
2"×12" GIRDER
F
2"×4" GIRTS
2"×6"
G
2"×4"
T
2"×4" GIRTS
CC
2-2"×6" (TREATED) SKIRT BOARD
Z
14'-2"

Top dimensions: 4¼" 2'-2¼" 10'-5½" 2'-0" 10'-5½" 2'-2¼" 4¼"

Pole building front wall framing *(above)*.   Pole building rear wall framing *(below)*.

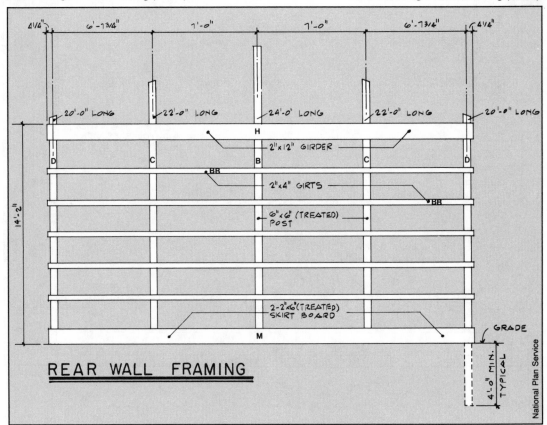

REAR WALL FRAMING

Labels visible in figure:
20'-0" LONG
22'-0" LONG
24'-0" LONG
22'-0" LONG
20'-0" LONG
D
C
B
C
D
H
2"×12" GIRDER
BB
2"×4" GIRTS
BB
6"×6" (TREATED) POST
2-2"×6" (TREATED) SKIRT BOARD
M
GRADE
4'-0" MIN. TYPICAL
14'-2"

Top dimensions: 4¼" 6'-7¾" 7'-0" 7'-0" 6'-7¾" 4¼"

Materials List
Pole Building

Key	Pcs	Size and description (use)
A		3 cubic yards concrete (post footing)
B	3	6×6×288″ timbers (posts)
C	2	6×6×264″ timbers (posts)
D	14	6×6×240″ timbers (posts)
E	1	4×4×240″ timbers (posts)
F	11	2×12×192″ lumber (rafter supports)
G	2	2×12×192″ lumber (sliding door header)
H	3	2×12×168″ lumber (rafter supports)
J	2	2×12×96″ lumber (rafter supports)
K	2	2×6×216″ lumber (skirt boards)
L	1	2×6×216″ lumber (service door jamb)
M	4	2×6×192″ lumber (skirt boards)
N	4	2×6×168″ lumber (skirt boards)
P	2	2×6×168″ lumber (sliding door track)
Q	6	2×6×144″ lumber (sliding door rails)
R	4	2×6×144″ lumber (truss bearing block)
S	4	2×6×144″ lumber (girder blocks)
T	3	2×6×144″ lumber (sliding door jamb)
U	2	2×6×144″ lumber (overhead door girt)
V	2	2×6×144″ lumber (sliding door sides)
W	2	2×6×120″ lumber (truss blocks)
X	2	2×6×120″ lumber (overhead closure)
Y	8	2×6×96″ lumber (truss knee brace)
Z	6	2×6×96″ lumber (skirt boards)
AA	42	2×4×206″ lumber (purlins)
BB	24	2×4×192″ lumber (girts)
CC	12	2×4×168″ lumber (girts)
DD	15	2×4×144″ lumber (truss bracing)
EE	2	2×4×144″ lumber (sliding door jamb)
FF	9	2×4×120″ lumber (diagonal braces)
GG	8	2×4×120″ lumber (cross bracing)
HH	4	2×4×120″ lumber (overhead door jamb)
JJ	2	2×4×96″ lumber (brace spacer)
KK	2	1×4×144″ lumber (sliding door trim)
		60′ molding (door stop)
		60′ metal corners
		40′ aluminum rake edge
		40′ vented ridge cap
		18′ molding (service door stop)
	1	28′ sliding door track & hardware
	1	36×80×1¾″ service door
	3	3½×3½″ door butts
	2	10×10′ overhead doors and hardware
	109	32×168″ aluminum panel (siding)
	5	32×144″ aluminum panel (door siding)
	64	32×96″ aluminum panel (roofing)
	6	32×72″ plastic roof panel

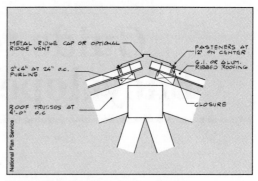

Pole building ridge construction detail.

Next, install roof purlins 24-in. o.c., butted over trusses. Space them at the ridge for the vented ridge cap.

Install aluminum or galvanized ribbed roofing panels beginning at a lower corner farthest away from the direction of the prevailing wind to minimize wind damage. Overlap sides 1½ corrugations and ends 6 to 9 inches. Fasten at least 1 in. into the purlins using galvanized 2¼-in. screw-shank nails with neoprene washers.

Construct wall girts next using the 2×4 temporary pole bracings. Install 2×6-in. skirt boards as shown. Then install siding and doors. Finally, trim eaves and corners. Your pole building is complete.

You can modify this pole building to serve a variety of purposes: You can construct walls to separate areas into bays; you can add stalls for larger animals; you can put in a loft; add more doors to allow equipment or large vehicles to drive through.

Check Building Codes

Before you start building any project in this book, be sure to check local building code requirements. Don't rely on second-hand information about codes in your local area. Building codes vary in each local jurisdiction. Some of the plans given here may not be complete enough to satisfy requirements of local codes for construction. Check with local authorities, a structural architect or a building contractor before starting any outdoor structure project.

Additional Help

The material in this book expands on specific instructions and projects that you'll find throughout the 27 volumes of your *Popular Mechanics Do-it-Yourself Encyclopedia.* Review the material in your *Encyclopedia* to brush up on your basic building skills, review your knowledge of tools and construction techniques and look for other outdoor structure projects you can build. There is a guide to projects in the *Encyclopedia* beginning on page 124.

Guide to Related Encyclopedia Articles

Use this guide to locate related material in the 27-volume *Popular Mechanics Do-it-Yourself Encyclopedia*. You'll find other projects related to outdoor structures, helpful hints in using tools and materials and other information that will make your outdoor project easier to build.

In the listings given below, you are shown both the volume number and page number where that information appears in the *Encyclopedia*. For example, 12/1424 means that you'll find the section about **Hand Tools** in Volume 12, beginning on page 1424.

Index

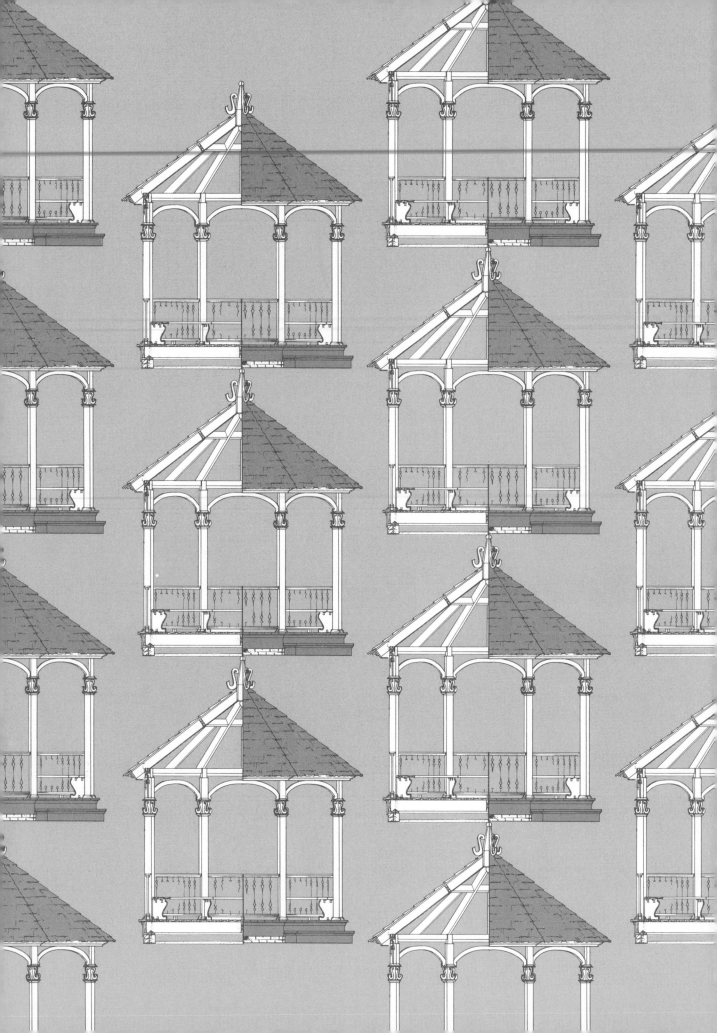